Rules for
the Southern
Rulebreaker

DISCARD

Rules for the Southern Rulebreaker

Missteps and Lessons Learned

Katherine Snow Smith

SHE WRITES PRESS

Copyright © 2019 Katherine Snow Smith

All rights reserved. No part of this publication may be reproduced, distributed, or transmitted in any form or by any means, including photocopying, recording, digital scanning, or other electronic or mechanical methods, without the prior written permission of the publisher, except in the case of brief quotations embodied in critical reviews and certain other noncommercial uses permitted by copyright law. For permission requests, please address She Writes Press.

Published 2019
Printed in the United States of America
ISBN: 978-1-63152-858-3
ISBN: 978-1-63152-859-0
Library of Congress Control Number: 2020901197

For information, address:
She Writes Press
1569 Solano Ave #546
Berkeley, CA 94707

She Writes Press is a division of SparkPoint Studio, LLC.

Interior design by Tabitha Lahr
Illustrations by Alli Arnold

All company and/or product names may be trade names, logos, trademarks, and/or registered trademarks and are the property of their respective owners.

Names and identifying characteristics have been changed to protect the privacy of certain individuals.

R0457980679

DISCARD

For Melinda, my first storyteller

DISCARD

The Rules

(Table of Contents)

Foreword

*I*n this introduction, I'm supposed to write about the purpose and inspiration of this book. I'm supposed to tell you why you should spend $16.95 on it instead of buying another mojito at an expensive restaurant. But, as I'm supposedly a "rule-breaker," I'm going to start with what this book is not.

This book is not ten truths you need to know to live your best life. It's not about coming to terms with divorce or the loss of a sibling. It's not about the rewards of being a journalist. It's not about nurturing your kids or the evils of helicopter parenting. It's not a love letter to the South or hate mail to the North. It's not an ode to divorced moms, happily married moms, working moms, stay-at-home moms, older moms, younger moms, organized moms, or moms who repeatedly try to use their car's keyless entry remote to open the front door of their house.

I have been all of those moms at various times over the past twenty-plus years. I can't say I was any better at one stage than I was at another. I can say I tried my best at every stage.

This book is an honest account of times when I may have pushed limits or made rash decisions. The title of each chapter is a "rule" I broke. I think these essays show that there can still be good outcomes when you don't do what everybody expects you to do. I'm not advocating for irresponsible decisions or poor choices; I'm just saying that life is messy for all of us, and sometimes you can't play by the rules.

I promise I'm not self-absorbed. (Said the women who wrote a book about herself.) But friends, other writers, and bartenders (mostly bartenders) have told me I have an innate ability to see both the humor and the poignancy in many of life's experiences.

So, read what's happened to me and think of the times when you broke the rules, intentionally or accidentally, and then let yourself off the hook. Stop being so hard on yourself. Leave that to your neighbor down the street. The one whose kids told you their mom said they can't go barefooted all the time like you do because then their floors would be dirty, too.

And remember, a lot of people have your back, so let them know when you need them and have their backs when they need you. That's a rule you should never break.

1. Always Wear Sensible Shoes

*B*efore I even crossed the finish line of the long maze of metal detectors, my feet were throbbing. As I ascended the stairs to the main floor of the White House, I clutched the railing with both hands to pull myself up. Every step created more intense pain. Twenty minutes into the media holiday party, I had to lean against a wall of the East Room, shifting my weight from one miserable foot to the other. Surrounded by high-profile media figures, centuries-old portraits of George and Martha Washington, and silver tureens erupting with shrimp and snow crab, all I could do was constantly scan the dozen or so little gold tables praying I'd find a place where I could take a load off.

My black satin shoes were beautiful, but the heels were four-inch shards of glass, the intricate organza ruffle crossing my foot: barbed wire. A friend insisted I borrow them because they went so well with the black sweater with pleated organza sleeves I'd bought for the big night. I tried the ensemble on at her house the day before I left for Washington, D.C., and though it was the perfect pairing, I was wary of the high elevation.

"Just take some Advil right before you go to the party. That's what I always do," Stephanie advised me. At the time I didn't think of this as drugging oneself in the name of fashion. I only saw sheer genius.

The Advil, however, didn't do the trick. An epidural could not have lessened the severe pain from my toes to my spine as I hobbled through the most elegant night of my life.

I couldn't carry a drink, much less a conversation, because I needed complete focus and free hands for balance to stand upright. I didn't get to try any of Dolly Madison's orange pound cake or the silver dollar biscuits pricked with fork tines and filled with Virginia ham. Maternal instincts did briefly overcome the pain, and I managed to collect a stack of sugar cookies iced to look like First Dog Bo, complete with holly leaves on his red collar. I wrapped them in a napkin and stuffed them in my pocketbook to take home to my kids.

I was at the White House Media Christmas Party with Adam, my husband at the time, who was the political editor for the *Tampa Bay Times*.

About an hour into the evening, it was our allotted time to go to the Map Room and get a picture taken with the president and first lady. As we neared the front of the line a white-gloved Marine instructed: "You may call him Mr. President, and her, Mrs. Obama."

"Hello, Mr. President," I said, and then turned to the first lady and added: "Merry Christmas, Michelle." Oh yeah. I went there. I went right there. I mean, was I really expected to retain simple etiquette instructions for a whole thirty seconds? I acted like we were the oldest of friends getting together for the Secret Santa gift swap at the office. What's up, Shelly? Hey FLOTUS, have you been naughty or nice?

"I'm sorry," I blurted out.

"Oh, it's fine," she said as the photographer positioned my new bestie Michelle on the far left, then Adam, then me, then the president. Just as we smiled for our big moment, my left foot twisted, my knee gave way, I fell against the 44th president of the United States then headed backward.

"Don't worry. I got you," Barack Obama said as he hoisted me back up.

"I should not have worn these shoes," I managed to say. "They're a mile high. I borrowed them."

He leaned his tall frame over and gazed down at my feet.

"Oh, those are great shoes," he said, reassuringly.

"I'm glad you wore them," added the leader of the free world who sometimes doubled as my stylist.

Adam had planned to ask Obama a quick question during our photo op about the infamous hug the president shared with Florida's former governor Charlie Crist when he was visiting the Sunshine State to dole out stimulus money. Crist, who was a Republican at the time of the hug, ran against Marco Rubio for Senate and lost in the primary. He switched parties to become an Independent and lost again in the general election. His hug with Obama was used against him in ads and posters to symbolize a lack of conservative GOP values.

I had caused such a commotion with the near fall that Adam just smiled for the camera and kept moving without asking the question.

"Oh, yeah," I said, once I was steady on my feet. "Adam wanted to ask you if you feel bad about the hug with Charlie Crist."

"Adam," he called after my red-faced husband. "I do feel bad. I'm sorry he lost, because he's a great guy."

Adam would recount the incident later, saying the Secret Service then pulled out their Tasers to get me out of the Map Room. We returned to the East Room and I had the best story of the night to share with fellow reporters. They may have been regulars in the White House Press Corps, but had President Obama ever complimented their shoes? Had he ever saved their life? As we left the White House, I took off my heels and carried them as I walked barefooted into the frigid D.C. night telling my story yet again to someone else who heard I'd fallen on the president.

Four years later, we were somehow invited back for another Obama holiday party. I wore sensible shoes with a ruby red dress. I called the first lady Mrs. Obama.

"Oh, what a nice, festive dress," the president commented as we posed for our photo. After the camera clicked, I started to ask him a question, but he'd already turned left to greet the next guest.

2. Children Require Age-Appropriate Entertainment

⁓

I'd never heard the words "ma'am" or "Molly" very often until I was the oldest attendee at the Okeechobee Music Festival in Central Florida a few years ago.

"You need any help with that tent, ma'am?" the guy with a turquoise tattoo of a deer's head and antlers blazoned across his chest asked as I struggled to build shelter out of some gray nylon and way too many plastic sticks.

"Where'd you get your necklace, ma'am? I love it," asked the girl selling peanut butter and jelly sandwiches that she'd apparently rubbed in the dirt and then jumped on five times.

"Sure, go ahead, ma'am. It's all good," said the shower attendee when I asked if he could please just let me in for free after learning I had to walk two miles to the General Store to buy a $7 token for admission to his portable showers.

As for Molly, that's the nickname for methylenedioxymethamphetamine, a close cousin of Ecstasy, and the drug of choice at music festivals these days.

"Hey, dude, did you score some Molly?" a clean-cut blond boy in a T-shirt that read "Good at Making Bad Choices" asked a guy wearing no shirt at all.

"Who the hell even gave us that Molly last night?" I overheard a girl camping near our tent ask her friends.

I didn't go to the music festival three hours away in the middle of Florida by choice. The only thing my then-seventeen-year-old daughter Charlotte wanted for her birthday was to go to Okeechobee Fest with her friend Samantha. Me tagging along in my turquoise Lilly Pulitzer shift and tortoise shell readers certainly wasn't part of her birthday fantasy, but nobody under eighteen was allowed admission without an adult.

"What? Are you running for mom of the year?" a friend asked when I told her I was taking the girls to Okeechobee.

"Or worst mom of the year," a frenemy chimed in with a smile, revealing her overly whitened teeth.

"Well, if you feel comfortable taking them, I think it's great. I just know I couldn't throw my daughter into all that at her age," another mom said or, rather, judged.

Enough with the judgment. I wasn't taking Charlotte and Samantha to turn tricks by the swamp or cook meth in an abandoned shack. We were camping in the great outdoors, unplugging, bonding, and seeing some great musicians.

The three-day lineup included Mumford and Sons, the Avett Brothers, Jason Isbell, the legendary Preservation Hall Jazz Band from New Orleans, and Kendrick Lamar. After arriving Friday evening, an attendant reeking of pot inspected my Honda Pilot for drugs, and we followed a line of cars rolling across grassy fields until we finally pulled in next to a grove of queen palms and managed to put up a four-man tent on our allotted swath of dirt. Charlotte and Samantha headed out in their jean shorts and embroidered, bell-sleeved shirts to see a rapper called Lil Dicky while I went to Hall & Oates.

"Sara Smile" made me smile. "Rich Girl" brought back memories of the twelve-year-old me listening to my transistor radio in my old tree house, hoping my mother wouldn't overhear the lyrics "It's a bitch girl."

Fast-forward thirty-six years and here's what my seventeen-year-old daughter was hearing at the Lil Dicky show. I don't have the rights to share the exact lyrics but one of his songs makes the point that he still hasn't "been up inside" a certain girl "before," but he really wants to have intercourse with the "whore."

Not only was my seventeen-year-old daughter listening to this, and plenty that was worse, I drove three hours and was peeing in the woods to enable her to hear it. As I fell asleep in the tent that first night, I tried to convince myself that liking music depicting wild behavior doesn't mean you engage in wild behavior. At her age, I knew every line of Prince's "Darling Nikki," yet I definitely did not become Nikki.

The next morning when the girls and I were using Neutrogena makeup wipes to clean off the dirt caked around our polished toenails, I thought of the advice those child psychiatrists on the *Today* show were always spewing about bringing up the tough topics.

"So . . . a lot of wild people here. Did you see the girl wearing only Band-Aids over her nipples?"

"That's, like, ridiculous," said Samantha.

"It's like, is a bikini really just too confining?" Charlotte added.

"And some people are just clearly so out of their minds on drugs," I said.

"We saw a girl throwing up in the middle of a mosh pit and none of her friends were even paying any attention to her," Samantha said.

"She looked so miserable. This would be the worst place to be so sick. There are no bathrooms. Gross," Charlotte said. "That made me never want to get that sick."

"You'd never want to get that sick at a music festival or anywhere?" I persisted.

"Nowhere, Mom. Okay?" Charlotte said with a smile and roll of her brown eyes. "I mean, most of the people here aren't totally drunk or messed up. It's more about music than getting messed up."

She was right, and I felt better. I was glad the "dialogue was started," to quote the experts.

Lil Dicky would also redeem himself when he later became a spokesman for Trojan condoms and safe sex. Here's what he had to say for guys who shun protection: "Let's talk about the potential consequences of that 'you got up in there raw' sex. Texting your friends about it. Ejaculated inside of her fully satisfied. I hope you're satisfied. How does it feel to go to work tomorrow with HIV?"

Give 'em hell, Dicky.

The second day of the festival, I was reading in the sun next to our tent when a neighboring camper, the one wondering where the hell that Molly came from, walked over to offer me a chicken and pesto wrap. It had been growing bacteria in the sun for hours and was the last thing I'd eat, and I'm someone who has eaten my fair share of pizza crusts out of the trash the day after my kids' sleepovers. But I didn't want to dampen her effort at camaraderie.

"That's so nice of you. Sure. I think I'll save it for dinner."

"It's, like, ten bucks."

"Actually, no thanks. I hit the grilled cheese food truck pretty hard at lunch."

Stacey didn't make a sale, but she still stayed to chat a bit. I learned she was in college in her native Maryland.

"It's my spring break so I'm here with some people I met at a music festival in Virginia last summer," she said. "The best festivals have so much variety in music, so you get a big variety of people. You can walk through and it's like listening to a radio station that's changing everywhere you go. I love finding new bands and new people."

I complimented her pendant, a stone wrapped in wire, hanging around her neck.

"It's a caged crystal. I gave my mom one just like it for Christmas, so I always feel close to her whenever I wear it," she said, clutching the jagged purple rock. "She's, like, my hero."

Fifteen minutes later, I overheard my new friend back at her tent informing everyone: "If I don't find drugs, drugs find me."

What would Stacey's mom back in Maryland wearing the matching caged crystal do if she heard that? Ban music festivals? Quit paying her college tuition? Ship her off to rehab?

Most of us moms just do the best we can, learning with each new situation along the way, making up the lyrics as we go.

3. Know Your Limitations

For two brief periods in my life, I was a competitive athlete. I thought I peaked in second grade when I ran the obstacle course faster than any other girl my age at J. W. York Elementary's field day, but I experienced a physical renaissance in my late thirties and ran a 5K every month or so for almost a year. Maroon 5's *Songs About Jane* album and the soundtrack from *Chicago* put Lance Armstrong's steroids to shame as adrenaline raged through my mind and legs, enabling me to run a fourteen-minute mile.

Still, when my friend Sally asked me to sign up for a duathlon with her, I quickly said no, then asked what a duathlon was.

"You run three miles, bike ten miles, then run another three," she explained.

"Well, then, *hell* no. You know I can barely run three miles, much less bike ten more and run again after the first three."

"Oh, come on," she said. "Don't you want to push yourself?"

"If I wanted to push myself, I wouldn't have begged for an epidural when I was thirty-seven weeks pregnant and my doctor said the baby might come within a week or two."

"Listen, we'll run the first three, then take a leisurely bike ride on a completely flat Florida road, then we can walk the last three. Come on, you'll be fine."

"This is ridiculous, but okay, if you promise, pinky swear, to walk the last three with me without even suggesting we run."

She put out her pinky, we sealed the deal, and as simply as that I became a duathlete in training.

I somehow had yet another overachieving friend, Helen, who loved to bike and ran marathons but had enough redeeming qualities that I couldn't hate her. She became my training coach, and we biked three times a week on the Pinellas Trail until I could manage eight miles without resting.

"Those last two will come easy on the day of the race," Helen assured me. "You'll be able to smell the pizza at the finish line."

"No, after I bike ten, I'll still have three miles after that before I get to the finish line."

"Oh, yeah. I cannot believe you signed up for this thing. What the hell are you thinking?"

Two days before the big event, I walked our basset hound, Delbert, past Sally's house and noticed kayaks on top of her minivan as she loaded a duffel bag in the back seat.

"Are y'all going somewhere, Sally?"

"Oh, yeah. I was about to call you, Katherine. The boys don't have school Monday, so we are going up to the river house for the weekend."

"What about the duathlon, Sally? The one you begged me to do with you."

"Well, I knew you didn't really want to do it, so I didn't think you'd care if we bagged it."

"Are you kidding me? I've trained. I'm ready. I'm in the best shape of my life. I can taste victory."

At that instant I knew how Carl Lewis felt when President Carter boycotted the Moscow Olympics in 1980. Lewis went on to win lots of gold in '84, but I knew I would only go downhill fast once my opportunity to shine passed.

"I'm still going to do it," I told Sally.

"Good for you. You'll have fun."

The annual Chilly Willy Duathlon at Fort De Soto Beach was the antithesis of fun. As I parked my three-gear bike in the transition area, a voice over a loudspeaker reminded any competitors who weren't members of the USA Triathlon Association to hustle on over to Tent B and sign an insurance waiver. I was one of three people out of about 200 competitors hustling to Tent B.

"I am going to kill Sally," I said to the other pitiful novices signing waivers with me.

One minute after a gun fired to start the race, I was at the back of the pack with a little boy and a man with an artificial leg. My mind flashed back to instructional swim at Camp Seafarer when I was fourteen. While my cabinmates were taking diving and water ballet, I was learning basic strokes along with Sarah, the last born of triplets who had learning disabilities, and Kumi from Japan, who didn't know how to swim or speak English.

As a duathlete, I should have reserved every bit of energy I could but decided if I started talking to the young boy next to me, he wouldn't pass me like the one-legged man did.

I found out Jason was ten years old but had been competing in races since he was five because his mom trains triathletes. His younger brother was named Race, because she ran a marathon while she was pregnant with him. My youngest son is named Wade after my grandfather, but also because I waded in the ocean a lot when I was pregnant with him.

The Chilly Willy was Jason's first duathlon, but he'd been in several triathlons because swimming was his best sport. Unknowing spectators along the race route gave me adoring looks and knowing smiles because I was the Best Mom Ever bringing up the rear with my son whom I was introducing to the great world of long-distance competition.

As we reached the transition area to mount our bikes, the first wave of competitors were already done with the bike sequence and heading to the beach to run the last three miles.

"We need to get moving," Jason said as he jumped on a lime green bike made of titanium, feathers, and marshmallows. I mounted my blue three-speed constructed of old railroad ties and rusty anvils. He left me in his dust, and I resigned myself to coming in last. There were plenty worse things, I told myself as I pedaled along the cracked asphalt road at Fort De Soto State Park. I was an able-bodied woman who could run and bike. I just couldn't do it quickly.

About this time, in the midst of my one-on-one therapy session with myself, I heard a car driving very slowly behind me as I reached the four-mile marker. I motioned for it to pass me, but it stayed on my tail. What a bush-league race. They couldn't even keep cars from driving on the course. The USA Triathlon Association ain't so great after all. I swung my right arm out wide again and motioned for the car to just pass me, but it refused. Finally, I turned around and saw a police car with lights flashing.

"Oh, God, please no," I said aloud, talking to myself, for the second time that day. The safety car was on my ass, making sure I didn't topple over or pass out in the heat. Helen would later try to make the best of it.

"At least he didn't have the siren blaring," she offered, "and be glad you hadn't been drinking."

For the next six miles, my personal escort followed more closely than the L.A. cops tailed O.J.'s white Bronco. I tried to salvage a shred of self-respect and come up with some nugget of wisdom I'd garner from coming in last in the Chilly Willy Duathlon.

"Never listen to Sally again" would have been a good lesson learned, but that was a moot point because I was going to drive up to her cabin and crush her with my bike later that night. So, I decided I had a lesson for my kids about coming in last and holding my head up high. I'd just seen a girl about eight years old a few days earlier wearing a shirt that said "Always First Pick" and wanted to tell her mom, who had most certainly bought the shirt, she was contributing to the delinquency of a nightmare. What has happened to decorum? I agree kids don't need a trophy just for showing up at practice, but do we really want to raise a generation of blatant braggers?

I decided to ride with pride as the policeman followed me and willed myself to stop thinking about what he would tell his hot girlfriend when she asked what he did all day at work. Finally, thankfully, I finished the ride and just had an easy three-mile run on the beach between me and the finish line. I could see Jason and the one-legged man way ahead in the distance, but there was no hope of catching up with them. I walked and ran in the slippery sand until I finally crossed the finish line as race organizers were throwing away the pizza boxes and packing up equipment.

A few days later I told a friend I'd come in last, but he had a hard time grasping the concept of "last."

"But you weren't dead last?"

"Dead last," I assured him.

"Just last for your age group, you mean?"

"Last for any age group. Last of the females, last of the males. Last of the humans. Last of the mammals. I saw a little squirrel skirt across that finish line just ahead of me."

"I would have paid good money to see that. Like real cash. There's got to be a video somewhere," a longtime childhood friend said when I recounted the story at my twentieth high school reunion.

"They should have left you a pizza to take home," my cousin laughed when I shared my tale with her at the annual Snow Reunion.

"Will you please tell the story about when you finished that race in last place?" a friend asked me at a Girls Night Out not too long ago.

Turns out, if you don't come in first, you might as well be last. It beats being in the middle of the pack.

4. Don't Major in Journalism

My lucky number has been twenty-three since the moment in 1982 when Michael Jordan took the winning shot in New Orleans that won Carolina the NCAA championship against Georgetown. The freshman from Wilmington, N.C. wore the number twenty-three and it's served him and me pretty well ever since. Jordan went on to win six NBA championships, amass a net worth of $1.9 billion, and become a leading philanthropist and a living legend.

As for me, I almost always come closest to the number someone is hiding behind their back when I guess twenty-three. I've also never had my debit card, Weight Watchers membership, or Netflix account hacked with the number twenty-three as part of my password.

The day after the Heels won it all, my parents let me miss a day of eighth grade and go to Chapel Hill for the welcome home celebration at Kenan Stadium. It was the most productive school day to date, because that's when I decided to work as hard as I could to get into Carolina.

Four years later, I got in early decision, which not only took the pressure off my senior year, but also determined my freshman roommate who I didn't know very well at the time but would become a lifelong friend. Since Beth and I both got in early, we applied to live together in Spencer and thought we had a good shot at a coveted room in the 1924 brick dorm with dormer windows right on Franklin Street. Turns out I got in no problem. Problem was, my roommate was someone I'd never heard of named Katie Turner.

Beth's housing application got lost in the mail, a.k.a. the kitchen counter. At the time, I couldn't understand how in the world her mother could miss such a crucial step in our lives. Thirty-two years later, when I took my own daughter to the accepted students' weekend at the University of Vermont a day late because I was looking at the school's online calendar of events for the previous year, I understood exactly how these things happen.

Beth ended up in Winston dorm in the middle of campus with a twenty-eight-year-old study abroad student from Germany named Lutzia. She came to Chapel Hill with four changes of clothes, one towel, and an intense desire to get a top-rate education. She was perfectly nice, but wasn't interested in matching comforters from Bed, Bath & Beyond, splitting the cost of a mini-fridge, or accompanying Beth to the Get Lei'd party in Winston's lounge.

My roommate Katie was nice girl with long blond hair and an easy laugh, but she spent most days and nights at her boyfriend's house, and I could go a week without seeing her. I was never lonely, however, because Bunny, the rabbit Katie gave her boyfriend for his birthday, lived in our room at Spencer. The boyfriend was scared his dog might kill it, so I was stuck with Bunny, and her smelly cage. At least the boyfriend seemed to appreciate me taking the hit and introduced me to several of his good-looking friends who became counterparts throughout Carolina.

One morning when I was taking Bunny's soiled newspapers to the garbage, I heard about an empty single room on the fourth floor of Spencer. Beth applied for a housing transfer and got it. I helped her move out of Winston dorm and witnessed the awkward farewell to her roommate. Beth removed Lutzia's food from the mini-fridge she was taking with her and placed it on a desk. She unplugged the fan she was taking with her and the temperature soared ten degrees on the hot September day. She took down the Claude Monet Water Lilies print (requisite of all freshmen girls in 1986) and left behind cold, bare walls.

"Well, I think that's it," Beth said. "Lutzia, call me if you need anything."

"I can't," she replied. "You are taking the telephone with you."

We were navigating roommates, classes, boys, budgets, and beer, so I'm glad we didn't have to decide our career path at age eighteen as well. Unlike today's students, who seem to start taking classes in their major before they pop their first middle-school pimple, I didn't declare my major until I was a junior.

Michael Jordan convinced me to go to Carolina. Darrin Stephens convinced me to major in advertising. Andrew Young, Eudora Welty, and Jim Shumaker turned me into a journalist.

Even before I decided I longed to go to UNC, Darrin Stephens, the bewitched husband of Samantha, got me interested in the world of advertising. It was creative and involved words, art, thinking on your feet, and entertaining clients. Three decades before *Mad Men's* Don Draper added power, sex, and money to the equation, I was intrigued.

So, when it came time to declare my major, I went with advertising, which was part of the School of Journalism at UNC. I started my junior year walking the same halls my father walked forty years earlier as a returning solider from World War II. He was glad I was following his path but not walking directly in his footsteps.

"Katherine, just don't major in journalism. You'll never make any real money. Advertising pays much better," said the man who grew up with very little, became editor at one of the South's leading newspapers, published four books of columns, and still worried about his retirement years.

I heeded his warning and settled happily into my advertising curriculum, spending hours creating romantic storyboards for a commercial about a young couple engaging in a snowball fight that quickly soils the heroine's white, wool sweater. But no fear, they tromp hand-in-hand to a cabin in the woods where Woolite and the gentle cycle save the day.

For an assignment on Jaguar, I turned in a sketch of Mick Jagger standing in front of the beautiful sports car and the slogan: "Mick Jagger wouldn't sing 'I Can't Get No Satisfaction,' if he drove a Jaguar." I got a D because the budget I was allowed for the fictious campaign didn't come close to affording Mick Jagger.

Around the time that I was getting no satisfaction from my advertising classes, I became more committed to the journalism class I was taking. Because the J-school offered advertising, public relations, and journalism, students were required to take one class in the two sequences that were not their major. Jim Shumaker, the inspiration for the Shoe comic featuring a cranky bird as a newspaper editor, taught, or rather terrorized the entry level students.

He locked the door the second the class started at 7:00 p.m. on Tuesday and Thursday nights. There was no need to knock or offer a pleading look through the narrow, vertical window in the door. If you were a mere ten seconds late, there was no entry and you received a zero for the class.

Mr. Shumaker was tall, with white eyebrows accenting his thick mustache of the same color, and had an almost bald head with a healthy tan from weekends at Topsail Island. His tough demeanor was lessened by his humor just enough to make students laugh, but not enough to make anyone feel safe.

Shu (as the cool kids called him) quickly distinguished the true journalism majors from the students taking his class because it was required by asking *Daily Tar Heel* staffers to raise their hands. Mr. Shumaker (as I called him) was tough on the journalism majors to make them better, he was tough on the rest of us just for sport.

A couple months into the semester, there was a Thursday night cocktail party that several classmates and I planned to attend. The other girls were just going to skip and take a zero, but I tried to get an excused absence.

"Mr. Shumaker, there's this cocktail party that's kind of a networking event Thursday night, and I was hoping to be allowed to miss class," I said to him as calmly as I could as we were leaving the Tuesday night session. He stared at me with a quizzical look but didn't unlock his fierce eyes from my face, which meant I was to continue.

"My date is actually working for a newspaper, his family owns several in North Carolina, so I might get tips for snagging an internship this summer," I stammered.

"Miss Snow. You had a B in my class and you now have a C for trying to garner favor with social connections. You have broken a cardinal rule of journalism," he said. "If you miss my class Thursday you will have a D." I went to class that Thursday night.

Shu held us to the highest of journalism standards for the stories we turned in to him each week. We were assigned breaking news, features, meeting coverage, and had to cover one ongoing issue throughout the semester. Somehow, I homed in on a debate within a Chapel Hill neighborhood where there were plans for six AIDS patients to move into a split-level house. This was 1989, five years before Tom Hanks would star in the groundbreaking movie "Philadelphia," which just started to chip away at homophobia and the sheer terror many Americans felt about AIDS. So even in a liberal college town like Chapel Hill, residents were wary of a respite for AIDS patients.

I interviewed the homeowners who didn't want a house full of people with a deadly illness they didn't understand, parents of twenty-something sons who were ill and couldn't get the care they needed at home, and the patients themselves. I wrote fair and probably overly emotional stories that nobody read but Shu.

His curriculum also dictated we cover two public speakers. I first wrote a story on civil rights icon Andrew Young, who was mayor of Atlanta at the time, when he addressed a packed house at UNC's Memorial Hall. Hearing him talk about death threats he received in the 1950s for organizing voter registration drives, made racism more real than anything I'd read in books.

Eudora Welty took the stage at Memorial Hall a few weeks later. The revered author, who won a Pulitzer Prize for *The Optimist's Daughter* in 1972, was very funny and very human.

The same week, my team in an advanced advertising class had to develop a campaign for another luxury car. We came up with "Saab. Why not?" The next day I switched my major from advertising to journalism and applied for a job at *The Daily Tar Heel*.

My first front page story broke the news that the speed limit was about to change on a major road from campus to many apartment complexes where students lived. The headline read: "Slow your speed on Airport Road," and I was teased for a week for being so bossy. I learned two things: people love to criticize reporters, and reporters shape conversations.

My father was right, of course. I didn't get rich as a reporter and was always counting the days until that next paycheck arrived. I covered plenty of routine occurrences and some downright boring and seemingly pointless meetings. I also broke a lot of news and wrote about amazing, yet everyday people.

"I'm so lucky to have had a job that I loved, and that was different every day," my father told me recently when we were having lunch at The Raleigh Times bar and restaurant in downtown

Raleigh. "The news changed every day and the readers loved me and hated me. It was never boring."

At the time, he was ninety-five years old and still writing a column after starting his newspaper career seventy years earlier. I was a reporter for a mere thirty years but am just as grateful for my time on the job.

5. Don't Move to Podunk

In my first newspaper reporting job, I thought of those swim instructors who throw babies into a pool. The babies have to figure out how to swim to the side, all on their own.

I soon became jealous of those babies.

You see, they always had parents on sidelines who would jump in and save them if needed. And when the babies made it to the side of the pool, either on their own or with help, they were immediately wrapped in a warm, soft towel and their cushy life resumed. When I started working at the *Greenville News*, nobody was on the side of the pool making sure I didn't drown. And there was no going back to the easy life I had before.

The Band-Aid was ripped off three days after I graduated UNC and went from living in a house full of friends and taking a class or two between parties and strolls down Franklin Street to living alone in a duplex next to Sandy's Hair Shack in Greer, S.C., which was pronounced "Grrrrr" by Sandy and other locals.

While most of my friends were in corporate training programs in Charlotte, Atlanta, and New York or spending a gap year in London, I was covering three town councils, the school board, the water board, a power cooperative, and smalltime crime while living alone and working alone out of my little home on John Street. I took the entry-level job knowing I had to cover the three small towns of Duncan, Lyman, and Wellford between Greenville and Spartanburg. I was told it would be just a few months until I got a desk in the newsroom thirty miles away in Greenville; however, I wasn't told that the other Greer reporter who also worked out of her house and actually got to cover Greer had been there eighteen months already and was still waiting for a spot in the newsroom. I'd move up to her job when she moved up to the newsroom. I also wasn't told my old clunky computer would have a screen the size of an index card and my editor in Greenville didn't want me to bother him unless I heard the words "rate increase" or couldn't get all my requisite seventeen weekly stories in on time.

My salary was $16,500. More than half of my paycheck went to Southern Bell because I regularly racked up $77 calls to London hearing my former college friends prattle on about crazy times on the Tube while chasing a party or falling asleep in the dressing room at Harrods, where they occasionally worked.

I'd like to say the fact that I was hot in Wellford buoyed me, but it didn't. Decades before Valerie Bertinelli and Betty White realized they were average in New York but *Hot in Cleveland*, I went from being an okay-looking coed in Chapel Hill to quite the head-turner in rural South Carolina. Honking horns from speeding pickups were customary as I took morning walks on country roads strangled in kudzu. Whistles in the Stop-N-Shop parking lot from pimply high school boys buying beer underage were a given. That first phone call from Tater, however, caught me off guard.

"Hello," I answered late one Saturday night.

"Hey, girlie," a male voice said.

"Hey. Who is this?"

"It's me."

"Who is me?"

"Geez. It's Tater," he revealed, frustrated I didn't instantly recognize the voice of someone I'd never once spoken to outside of the Wellford Police Department. Tater was the junior officer on the two-man force.

"Oh. Okay. Is something happening? Is there a murder or a drug bust?"

"Hell if I know. I'm not working. What are you doin'?"

"I'm not working either," I said.

"So what are you doin'?"

"Uh, nothing. What are you doing?"

"Talkin' to you."

"I guess you're right about that. Did you have a good weekend?"

"It ain't over yet. You goin' boggin' with me tomorrow?"

"What? What's boggin'?"

"Boggin.' Mud boggin'. A bunch of us are taking our trucks and some girls. You goin' with me?"

"Thanks for asking, but I can't." *I'd rather be sticking shards of glass under my fingernails while I spend $89 to call my friends and hear about their brilliant weekend.*

"Why not? You scared?"

Yes, I am. I'll admit I'm a little scared that a cop who I've heard use the n-word multiple times is calling me drunk at night and asking me out, and I'm saying no though I don't want to alienate him because I rely on him for news tips.

"I'm not scared of a little mud. I just have a lot of errands to do tomorrow, and then there's church, you know, of course, and I'm having lunch with my friend's parents in Greenville and then going to the library there. But thanks for asking."

"Library? Geez. Okay. Bye."

Tater never asked me out again. He also never made eye contact again or gave me any extra details beyond the scant information scrawled on police reports of DUIs, home invasions, and dog bites.

But Doris more than compensated. She called herself a retired housewife because her husband had died a decade earlier and her only daughter was grown and out of the house. She knew everyone and everything, and everything that everyone was doing. Doris told me about the five-year-old boy in Duncan who begged his daddy to build him a little wooden church instead of a treehouse, and the ninety-year-old woman in Wellford who grew more azaleas in her sprawling yard than anyone else in Spartanburg County. She was the authority on who hated whom on the school board and which mayors skipped church. Thanks to Doris, I landed my only front-page story in sixteen months at the *Greenville News*.

"Katherine, honey, you need to get over to the Lyman post office pronto," she said when she called one day, waking me from my afternoon nap in my home office. "Somebody is mailing a live bird to California."

I wrote the epic story on my three-by-five-inch screen, inserting a couple of obligatory puns, courtesy of my father. It was "poultry in motion" that didn't "ruffle any postal feathers" because mailing birds with proper ventilation was permitted.

It was also Doris who told me about a divorced mom who was telling people she had to have sex with a local police officer to get out of a DUI.

"My son has a lot of medical issues, and I can't afford to lose my license or my job. It's just me," Lisa told me, off the record, at her apartment between rapid drags on her Marlboro Lights.

It was a new police officer from the other side of the state who just started on the force. Lisa had had about three beers after work because her son was spending the night with a friend. She probably did swerve a little, so she begged the officer as soon as he approached her window with the long, silver flashlight not to give her a ticket, or could he at least make it a speeding ticket, because her son had special needs and she couldn't lose her license.

"He asked me if my back seat folded down. He said if I cooperated, I didn't have to get any ticket at all," Lisa told me without a tear as she reached for her fourth cigarette. She knew what he meant and begged him to just drop the ticket, but he said there was only one way out. So Lisa climbed in the back of her car and let it happen.

Afterward, she told a few people and learned this officer was trying the same justice system with other women. She was mad, and that's why she agreed to talk to me. I was mad, too, and convinced her that a story in the newspaper could get him fired and help her case if she pressed charges. Lisa agreed to tell me everything again on the record while I recorded her on tape.

The next day, I asked the police chief for records of any complaints about his newest officer. He knew of none. I called my editor in Greenville, reminded him who I was, and actually got invited to come to the newspaper's tall home office in downtown Greenville and play the tape for him and the managing editor. They were intrigued greatly, but said I needed to find another woman to go on the record saying the same thing happened to her before I could write anything. Late that afternoon Doris called to say the police officer had been fired.

"No, no, no, he wasn't fired," the mayor told me with a chuckle. "He's moving away. To Alabama or maybe Florida. He has a brother or a cousin down that way."

I requested copies of every traffic ticket the officer had written, hoping to find someone who opted for a ticket and fine over sex. I called about thirty women, most of whom didn't want to talk to a reporter. A couple said the officer was kind of creepy, but they weren't propositioned. Several hung up before I could even finish my awkward question.

Lisa called me regularly for a while asking if there was going to be a story, but all I could do was ask how her son was doing and tell her I was sorry. I moved to Charlotte a few months later to take a job with the *Charlotte Business Journal*. I carefully packed the cassette tape with Lisa's story in the top drawer of the wooden jewelry box my Aunt Zetta gave me for high school graduation.

There was nothing I could do with it, but I couldn't get rid of it.

6. Don't Talk to Strangers

Somewhere along the way, between invites for mud bogging and corrupt police officers, I covered my first night of election returns. Even neophytes like me were assigned to the county courthouse where the vote tallies came in and were projected up on a big screen. It was very high tech, like in high school when teachers put math equations or anatomical drawings on an overhead projector.

Reporters from local TV, the *Greenville News*, and our competition, the *Spartanburg Herald-Journal*, gathered there until midnight to watch and report the returns. One of the few reporters I knew at the *Greenville News* introduced me to several reporters from the Spartanburg paper.

"Where is your office?" one asked me.

"In my living room," I said. "I work out of my house."

"So, what's happening on *All My Children*?" another reporter named Adam Smith asked.

"Adam Chandler's long-lost twin, Stuart, has been living in the attic for forty years, apparently," I said and went on to share the perks of working from home in my pajamas since this was long before telecommuting was even a term, much less the norm.

Later that night, Adam stood next to me as I deciphered the numbers on the big screen and scribbled them in my notebook. I'm lucky he was looking over my shoulder.

"I think you are confusing the number of votes with the number of precincts because I'm pretty sure your candidate has more than twenty-eight votes this late in the night," he told me.

"I have absolutely no clue what I'm doing. Thank you so much," I blurted out. "Can you just write the whole story for me, and I'll pay you my daily wage of $10?"

We talked more when all the reporters went out to a bar after our stories were filed, and I learned Adam had been in Spartanburg about a year after working at a paper in Salisbury, a small town outside of Charlotte.

He asked me out the next weekend, and it was then that I realized he had worked in Salisbury, Connecticut, not Salisbury, North Carolina. Adam was actually from New York City. I was on a date with real live Yankee!

I learned his dad was from Mobile, Alabama, and his mom was from Chicago, so I reasoned I could make it through dessert. We made it longer, actually, and were married twenty-four years before an amicable divorce.

But back when we started dating in South Carolina, three months in he invited me to go to New York to meet his parents. Well, that wasn't the intent of the trip, but it was a side effect that had me all nervous. We were actually going there because his parents were friends with Hal Gurnee, who was the director of *Late Night with David Letterman* at the time. They had four tickets to see the show. Adam, having just come off a three-year relationship, told me he wasn't ready to get serious and this was not the "meet the parents" weekend.

I guessed his parents were wondering how their son had latched on so quickly to a girl in Greer, S.C., and I worried they preferred him with someone more worldly, who'd gone to a New England liberal arts school and could quote Proust instead of

Margaret Mitchell. I was intimidated but determined to show I was smart and worldly, and my Southern charm was just the icing on the pound cake.

"Now they do know I'm from Raleigh and not Greer, right?" I asked Adam the night before we left. "And did you tell them I lived in London one summer and that this isn't my first time to New York and that I went to Washington, D.C., in fifth grade on a field trip for all the Safety Patrols?"

"Yes, yes, yes. They are fully aware of how cosmopolitan you are," he assured me. "But it really doesn't matter. We're only going to have dinner with them after the show. That's it."

Adam flew direct from Spartanburg to LaGuardia. But I used a free ticket I'd earned on Northwest Airlines the year earlier after being bumped off a spring break flight home from Jamaica. So, I took the airline's only path north: Spartanburg to Memphis to Detroit to Newark.

Three-fourths of the way into my connect-the-dots odyssey, the flight from Detroit to Newark was delayed. I called Adam's parents' house and spoke to his mom for the first time ever to ask her to relay the info to Adam if he called since I was meeting him at a hotel in the city.

"Okay. Well, thank you for letting us know and I'll let him know," she said. Was she annoyed? Did she like me? Did she hate me? I couldn't tell.

"So why are you going to Newark?" a cute guy sitting two seats away in the Detroit airport asked.

"I'm going to New York to meet my boyfriend for the weekend," I said, sounding so cosmopolitan it killed me.

"Well, I'm going to New York to meet my girlfriend. So there," he said, teasing me for no apparent reason. "I'm Marc Jaffe."

"I'm Katherine Snow. Are you from Detroit?"

"God no. New York. But I'm in law school at the University of Chicago."

"Where are you from?"

"Raleigh, North Carolina."

"I know one person in the whole world from North Carolina. I worked with a girl named Charla Price last summer at an ad agency in New York."

"No way. She's my cousin."

"You're kidding. What is she doing now?"

"I have no idea. I don't really know her."

I went on to tell him about my father's fourteen siblings and how there were a lot of relatives I didn't know. Charla's mom, Charlene, was actually my first cousin, and I adored her but had never met her daughter who was just a year my senior. She lived seven hours away, and we never visited Dobson, the town of our roots, at the same time.

"So, everybody in North Carolina is related," he said. "It really is just like *The Andy Griffith Show*."

"Wrong. And wrong. Not everyone in North Carolina is related; furthermore, nobody on *The Andy Griffith Show* was related except, of course, for Andy, Opie, and Aunt Bee. Well, actually, Goober and Gomer were cousins. But it wasn't the whole town."

"What's a Goober and a Gomer?"

"If you have to ask, you wouldn't understand. Just forget it."

"Gladly," he snapped, and then went on to tell me that along with seeing his girlfriend in New York he had an interview for a summer job at a law firm. I shared my plans, and he was actually impressed I was seeing *Letterman*.

"I still can't believe you don't know your own cousin. You must have a lot of cousins you don't know. You could potentially meet a guy in a bar, sleep with him, and inbreed without even knowing he was related to you?"

"You know what? You don't need to worry about whom I meet in bars or with whom I sleep because it doesn't concern you in the slightest."

"Ouch. Get back, Loretta," he laughed.

We were friends now. Throwing barbs and telling our life stories. He'd been dating his girlfriend for several years and planned to marry her but hadn't proposed. I confessed I was the somewhat nervous transitional girl meeting my boyfriend's parents for the first time, hoping I'd soon be out of transitional territory.

It was 1991, the midst of the first Gulf War, and loudspeakers at all three airports I'd frequented that day repeatedly warned travelers to watch their bags at all times. But now a new alert was blaring. Our flight to Newark was cancelled because of a looming snowstorm.

Marc and I rushed to a Northwest desk and learned there was a flight to Islip, N.Y., leaving in thirty minutes. It was the last chance to get out of Detroit for the weekend.

"Can I take a cab from Islip to Manhattan?" I asked him.

"Yeah, if you want to spend $500," he quipped. "But my parents live near Islip. I'll get their car and drive to the city tonight. You can ride with me, North Carolina, if you don't say anything else that stupid."

I had just enough time to call Adam's mom to update her and calmly said I was getting a ride from Islip to New York City with a guy I met at the Detroit airport.

"Katherine, do you feel safe with him?" she asked. "Do you think this is a good idea?"

I quickly explained that he had worked with my cousin, though I did not tell her I had never met my cousin. I added that Marc went to Harvard undergrad and was now in law school at the University of Chicago.

Her tone changed from skeptical to impressed.

"The University of Chicago is a *very* good law school. I'm sure you'll be fine."

By the time my well-pedigreed stranger and I landed in Islip, it was after midnight. Marc's father was waiting at the little airport.

"You're not driving into the city tonight," Mr. Jaffe told his son. "I'll take you in the morning when I go to the office."

"I've got my interview in the morning. I need to go tonight."

"You're not going this late, Marc."

They went back and forth for a while until the younger Jaffe said: "Well what about her?"

"Who?"

"The girl I met in the Detroit airport. I promised her a ride," he said, motioning to the pitiful figure a few feet away feigning great interest in the vending machine.

"I don't care about the girl you met on the plane. You aren't driving there tonight."

They argued a bit more in hushed tones as I stepped farther away, mortified, looking around to see if there was a hotel connected to Islip Regional Airport or perhaps just a broom closet where I could curl up for the night with a bottle of floor cleaner and my embarrassment. Marc finally came over to tell me we weren't going to the city until morning, but I could spend the night at his parents' house. Twenty minutes later, I was crawling into a double bed with his younger sister.

"Sarah, this is a friend of Marc's," his mom told her daughter, who was half asleep. "Her name is, um . . ."

"Katherine Snow," I offered.

"Scream if you need anything, Sarah."

The next morning, Marc's mother offered me a glass of orange juice as we stood in the kitchen and watched breaking news. Saddam Hussein had surrendered, and the Gulf War was ending.

Mr. Jaffe drove Marc and me into the city. The forty-five-minute car ride was mostly silent. Adam met me at the law firm where Marc was interviewing.

"Why didn't you tell me you wanted to go to Islip?" he asked.

That afternoon I met his parents at the *Letterman* show minutes before it started. I'd been dreading it all day because, well, I'd spent the night with a guy I met in the airport on the way to meet them and their son.

"Oh, Katherine, I'm so glad you made it," his mom said, giving me a hug.

"And I'm not sure you're better off with Adam instead of the law student," his father teased.

Letterman, being prodded by Hal Gurnee, spoke to me during his brief monologue to warm up the audience.

"Miss, are those suede pants you're wearing?" he asked. I nodded yes. "I've always wondered, don't they chafe you?"

His guests were Dana Carvey and Ashley Montana, who had just been on the cover of *Sports Illustrated*'s swimsuit issue. But at dinner afterward, it was Late Night with Katherine Snow. Adam and his parents and even Hal got a good laugh as I told my humiliating story of being stranded at the Jaffes and confessed I had never even met the cousin who my host knew.

"Katherine, you are so resourceful and brave," his mom said. "Anybody else would have been stuck in Detroit for the weekend."

"I'm not surprised this smart lawyer seized on the chance to save you from a weekend in Detroit," his dad added. Adam beamed. And just like that, my route from Spartanburg to Memphis to Detroit to the Jaffe household led me right out of transitional territory and into official girlfriend status.

—※—

7. Never Arrive at the Funeral Home Late

I watched from the second-to-last basement stair, which was covered in the original short-pile marigold carpet from 1959. My mother ironed my sister Melinda's tea-length dress. It was the color of orange sherbet, lace overlaying silk. Melinda had worn it to our cousin Melanie's wedding several years earlier. It would be the last dress she would ever wear, because she was to be buried in it the next day.

We had to be at Brown-Wynne Funeral Home to plan my sister's funeral in just about an hour. My mother, who painstakingly pressed every tuck and every pleat, was moving in slow motion. Then she stopped ironing to talk, a habit that always drove me crazy.

"First thing this morning, we heard a lawnmower and looked out the dining room window and that sweet Grady Cooper was mowing the lawn. He did the front and back in all this heat," she told me, referring to my dad's good friend since sixth grade. Grady knew we'd have people coming over and wanted the house to look good, but more so, he just wanted to do something to help when there really was nothing anyone could do.

"And then that wonderful Glenn Keever insisted on going with your father and Alean to the funeral home this morning," she said as she placed a tulip sleeve over the tip of the ironing board.

Alean was the housekeeper who had stayed with Melinda and me when we were little and my mother taught at N.C. State University. She was still coming once a week when Melinda died at age thirty-one in a car crash. After my father told her the funeral would be closed casket, Alean asked if she could see Melinda once more. He complied immediately, later telling me he wouldn't have done that for anyone but her.

Glenn was one of my father's closest friends. He had identified my sister's body for the authorities after she was killed by a drunk driver. My parents were out of town, and I was living in Florida. This all happened more than twenty years ago, and as every well-wisher promised me at the time, the pain has lessened. The gaping hole will never be refilled.

I still remember how the basement smelled that day with the stiff, clean fragrance of Niagara Spray Starch as my mom ironed. It was a familiar scent because the ironing board was always in our basement, where Melinda and I had spent hours, thousands of hours, playing. She was three years older, so she always directed whatever we were doing, but her unleashed imagination rarely gave me reason to complain.

My mother seemed to have lost five pounds in the three days since we had convened at our brick house in Raleigh following Melinda's death. Her yellow linen dress was a burlap sack on her as she stood at the ironing board. I had never seen her exercise beyond an evening walk, but ironing was an Olympic sport with lots of pounding and intricate turns on flowing fabric. Her hand was always quicker than the eye as she got anything ready to walk out the door within minutes looking much better than the day it was bought. Today, however, she was taking f-o-r-e-v-e-r. We were going to be late if she didn't pick up the pace.

To my right was the big brick fireplace, devoid of ashes in June. I pictured it two decades before, lined with produce boxes my mom procured from Winn-Dixie so Melinda and I could stack them three high and eight long to build empires for our Barbies. We created more than we'd played. The perfectly proportioned plastic dolls slept on lush beds made from Kleenex boxes and potholders. Lamps were Crest lids stuck on aggie marbles with Silly Putty. For chairs, we cut off the tops of Dixie cups, stuffed them with cotton balls, and covered them with scraps from the sewing cabinet.

Our next-door neighbor Marie Smith complained repeatedly to my mother that when she washed her dishes, she looked out her kitchen window down the hill into our messy basement full of boxes. Melinda and Katherine should clean up their toys at the end of each day like her daughter Betty had always done.

My mother put up curtains.

We had the requisite plastic Barbie furniture, too, and wooden ladder-back chairs Santa put in our stocking every year. Once we were old enough to know, Melinda teased my parents as she peeled the "Made by the Blind" stickers off the chairs and asked if Santa's elves were visually impaired.

Finally, my mother was done ironing Melinda's dress. She carefully hung it on a padded coat hanger. Now if she could just change clothes quickly we could leave in ten minutes and get to the funeral home almost on time. But then she placed a pair of white cotton underwear over the ironing board and gingerly touched the steaming iron to the fabric, an inch at a time.

Nobody, I mean nobody, was even going to see the underwear. What was she doing? And then I got it. I was only four months pregnant with my first child, but I got it. She wanted to be Melinda's mother for five more minutes. She wanted to keep ironing, caring, teaching, defending, celebrating, helping, consoling, praising. This was the last thing she would ever do for her daughter.

"I love you so, so much and so did Melinda," I said as I rushed to my mother and hugged her.

"Thank you, Katherine. I love you more than you will ever know," she said through tears.

We were a good half hour late to the funeral home. Nobody complained.

———

8. Don't Bring Your Problems to Work

~∞~

*E*very pregnant woman in the '90s received three copies of *What to Expect When You're Expecting* at her baby shower, even though she had already rushed out to by her own copy the day after she had unprotected sex for the first time. We had no Internet on which to look up questions and symptoms, so the book became an appendage the moment that second line on the plastic pregnancy test turned pink. Since we also had no Dr. Oz to warn us that constant self-diagnosis is a bad thing, we grew to hate the sketch of the serene mother-to-be confidently patting her belly on the book's cover, because she made us feel our constant worry meant we were already failing at motherhood.

Six weeks into my first pregnancy, my total lack of morning sickness convinced me my baby was completely cut off from my food supply. By eight weeks, I'd gained twice the weight I should have. At nine weeks, I was so behind on my Kegel exercises that a Caesarean section loomed as certain. At ten weeks, when my forehead felt clammy as I headed out the door to work, I knew it was critical that I discern if I had a fever, because I'd read something in *What to Expect* stating fevers can cause problems with the baby.

I was running late and faced a forty-five-minute commute from Tampa to the *St. Petersburg Times* bureau in New Port Richey, so I grabbed the glass thermometer out of the bathroom drawer filled with Q-tips and bobby pins, then stuck it in my mouth as I pulled out of the driveway. I planned to drive straight to the doctor's office if I had a fever, but before I reached the first stoplight, I found out I was a cool 98.6. I checked twice more to make sure, because you can't be too careful when you're maintaining a normal body temperature for two. Finally, I was satisfied my baby was safe, but, of course, I still failed as a mother because I didn't do a single Kegel exercise at a single stoplight as *What to Expect* suggested.

As I neared my office, I moved the glass thermometer from the passenger seat and dropped it into the lower compartment on the driver's side door. It sat there three days before I noticed that the heat had burst the glass and silver drops of mercury were oozing out.

"I've got mercury secreting in my car because I broke a thermometer," I said as I walked into the ten-person newsroom. "Is that bad or anything?"

"Only if you're pregnant," quipped my editor, Mike Moscardini. "It can cause birth defects."

I didn't make it the twenty feet past his desk to my own before wailing: "I am pregnant. Oh my God. What did I do?"

Fingers throughout the newsroom poised on A-S-D-F-J-K-L-; froze in place. Snarky banter went silent. A motley crew of work colleagues transformed into my greatest allies.

"How far along are you?" Moscardini asked.

"Ten weeks," I answered.

He fired off orders.

"Jamal, call whoever handles hazardous materials in Pasco County. Thomas, find the leading expert on the effects of mercury on unborn babies. Roger, get everything the CDC has on mercury and pregnant women."

I don't know what ran in the daily *Pasco Times* section the next day because everyone in our small but mighty troop was researching mercury or trying to comfort me. Normally, we were used to cranking out stories on crime, business, arts, education, and the typical bizarre Florida happenings that plagued Pasco County.

There was the owner of the German restaurant who kicked out a policeman for putting ketchup instead of applesauce on his potato pancakes; the all-you-can-eat-buffet restaurant patrons who saw nothing wrong with lining their pocketbooks with aluminum foil and taking food home for the rest of the week; the dinner theater director who caught flack for giving all the leading parts to his girlfriend, Candy Cane; and the neighborhood association president with the electric bullhorn warning "BUYERS BEWARE" as he walked behind a fast-talking vacuum cleaner salesman going door to door in a retirement community.

"If a vacuum cleaner costs $1,400, I want to be able to ride it to work," Moscardini said when I told him about the ruckus at Sunset Shores.

Ask anyone who ever worked for Mike Moscardini, including the reporters and editors who went on to win Pulitzers, cover the White House, or become editors at top papers and websites, to name the most influential journalist in their career and most of them will say: "Moscardini." We never called him Mike.

On the surface, he was an asshole. Underneath he wasn't. He had a great sense of humor and sincere interest in every story and every journalist. When a reporter heard a small-time circus was coming to Pasco and raising a big top in the dejected county for the first time in decades, Moscardini immediately instructed him to find a way to be fired out of the cannon on opening day and write a first-person story on it. "Even if it's your last," he added.

Moscardini gave no misleading pretenses that he'd be an easy boss starting from the job interview. I unknowingly went through the same rite of passage others before me were subjected to after going on about my passion for local news and exposing corruption. He nodded and even seemed moderately impressed with my clips.

"Well, this all sounds pretty good," he said. "But let me ask you, what do you make of Fawn Liebowitz?"

The name was familiar, but I had no idea who she was or what she had to do with Florida news or journalism.

"Um, I'm spacing. I'm not sure who you are talking about."

"You're not sure or you have no earthly idea?"

"I have no earthly idea."

"Well, have you ever heard of a little movie called *Animal House*?" he said in disgust and walked out of his office, leaving me sitting alone.

Still I wasn't totally shocked as I watched the hard-ass editor become my fiercest protector when crisis hit one of our own. Within less than an hour of the mercury discovery, the Pasco County Hazardous Materials division was well aware of the situation at the *St. Petersburg Times* bureau when I called to find out if it was okay to drive my car home at the end of the day.

"Oh, you're the pregnant lady at the *Times*. The one with the spill," the secretary said. "I'm going to put you right through to our director."

He advised me to go nowhere near said vehicle, not even to get the garage door opener or my copy of *What to Expect When You're Expecting*, and gave me a list of companies that handle hazmat cleanups. After sharing my story with the one nearest our office, the owner declined to take the job.

"Look, you being pregnant and all, I just can't be responsible for making sure the car is completely safe. If your baby comes out with two heads or something, you could sue the hell out of me," he said matter-of-factly as I burst into tears yet again.

After that, Mike assigned Roger to go down the list and soon he found a company in Lakeland, two counties to the east, that would tow my car to their shop and decontaminate it for $1,500. I had not thought to put a hazmat cleanup rider on my car insurance policy, so it was all out of pocket.

Two hours later a three-man crew showed up in yellow suits and clear helmets that I think they bought from the set of Dustin Hoffman's *Outbreak*, which had come out a year earlier. The advertising staff joined the news team in our executive editor Bill Stevens' office as we watched Pasco's hazmat trio rope off the parking lot with yellow hazard tape lined with skulls and crossbones. Then, in a death-defying instant, the bravest of the three opened the driver's side door, turned the ignition, put the car in neutral, and slammed the door shut. My red Volvo, the car we bought because it was the safest on the road until I turned it into a deathtrap, was hooked up to a waiting tow truck and transported seventy-five miles to Lakeland.

Moscardini broke the silence.

"That's it? That's all those clowns had to do?" he fumed. "Hell, I'd have let you pay Leo fifty bucks, and he could have held his breath and done that." Leo was Moscardini's twelve-year-old son.

By the end of the day, my colleagues learned of several case studies involving pregnant women and mercury. One of the four, a dental hygienist exposed to high levels of the element, gave birth to a baby with developmental delays. We learned that breathing mercury in its gaseous state, like I had, is much more dangerous than holding or even swallowing it in a liquid state. Like a true newsman and protector, Moscardini encouraged me to be tested so we could have all the facts. After a week of collecting my urine, keeping it in a cooler next to my desk, and hearing countless jokes about the smell of piss in the air, my ample sample was sent off to a lab. Five days later, we all learned I had as much mercury in my system as someone who had eaten swordfish several times in one week.

I say "we" found out, because it wasn't just me, it was the whole newsroom, who worried for me and with me.

About seven months later when Olivia was born, within minutes of scoring a ten on the Apgar, Roger called the hospital from the office for an update.

"It's a girl. They named her Olivia Snow Smith. She's completely healthy. And Katherine's fine, too," I heard him announce to the newsroom, with applause followed by laughter.

"Moscardini has one question," he relayed. "Can you still get your weekend story in by Friday at noon?"

—888—

9. Send Your Kids to the Best School in Town

*M*y oldest daughter was ready to start school from about the time she was two. She watched *Arthur*, the animated aardvark on PBS, win Mr. Ratburn's spelling bee and wanted to do the same. She loved the book, *Lilly's Purple Plastic Purse*, and acted out taking her own purple plastic purse off to school, where there were pointy pencils and rows and rows of books. She watched neighboring kids go to school each day only to return looking the same, but Olivia seemed to fear they were gaining on her.

After preschool, we signed her up for the private school at our Episcopal church. The close-knit campus completely won us over when we visited and watched students announce their good times and sorrows, ranging from losing a tooth to the death of a family pet, at the daily flag ceremony. A few months later when Olivia was a student, she proudly leaned into the microphone one day and said her basset hound, Delbert, had learned to play the xylophone; apparently, he dropped his bone on her brightly colored Fisher-Price instrument, and she just went with it. But by kindergarten we realized it was not a good fit for her after all. Fearing she might not complete her daily tasks, Olivia insisted on getting to school twenty minutes before the flag-raising to get an early start. I felt her pain when I took her in at noon after a dentist appointment and was handed a thick stack of worksheets she needed to make up after missing the first three hours of school.

My husband and I grew more concerned at a teacher conference when Mrs. Davis told us Olivia was confusing her lower- and upper-case letters on her A-B-C worksheets. Extra time with flashcards at home would help her catch up. She could suggest a tutor if we wanted to go that route.

The child was in kindergarten and already needed a tutor?

Mrs. Davis did share one bright spot, however, from a creative writing exercise the class had done the previous month during which they dictated a story based on an illustration of children riding a school bus. While most of the students espoused about the girl eating from her lunch box or the boys throwing a ball, Olivia zeroed in on the one dark-skinned student who was inserted by the politically correct curriculum publisher.

"John was nervous. He was the only black boy on the bus, and this was his first day of school. He wondered if there would be other black boys or girls at his new school. He was scared but also excited. He was ready to learn no matter what happened."

"I can't wait to hear what she will write next," Mrs. Davis said.

"When will they finish their stories?" I asked.

"Well, we hope to try another creative writing workshop after Christmas, but I'm not sure we'll have time."

By March, Olivia dreaded each day of school. This girl who was so outside the box was terrified of being caught veering outside the lines.

"You only have three more days until spring break," I told her one morning as I held up three fingers.

"But three days in Mrs. Davis' class are a lot longer than your fingers," she replied. I got into my car after the flag ceremony that morning and cried. In April, she answered the math problem that would change the course of her young life.

When asked to divide a square in half, Olivia drew a zigzag line right down the center. Mrs. Davis put a big red X across the square and made no effort to explain why Olivia's slightly different but potentially correct line of reasoning wasn't the right answer. The next day I called Sunflower, a Montessori-esque school near the beach in Gulfport, just southwest of St. Petersburg, and tried to make an appointment for Olivia to shadow.

"Well, we always like to talk to a potential student's parents first to make sure we'd be a good fit for the whole family before anyone visits," Nancy, the office manager, explained. Nancy wanted to see if we spoke the same anti-establishment, touchy-feely language, so I told her about the red X on the geometry question.

"We hear that kind of stuff a lot. We have one student who was taking a test or something at his other school and there was a sketch of a man without an arm. He was asked to fill in what was missing, and he drew a smile on the man's face," she said. "The teacher told him he should have drawn a second arm. Daniel is the kind of kid who thrives at Sunflower."

Olivia could thrive circles around Daniel, but we had to prove it to Nancy and the head of school, Marie, who also taught, drove on field trips, and likely sang backup for Peter, Paul and Mary in the '60s. My husband and I passed their nonjudgmental judging, and Olivia was invited to shadow for a day. Sunflower thrilled her, and she thrilled Sunflower. The worst part was telling her she had to wait until the beginning of the next school year to start going there.

Finally, the day came. Olivia arrived at Sunflower, took off her shoes, put them in her cubby, and joined all the other barefooted children for morning meeting.

"Can I bring in a bowl of spaghetti that feels like brains for the haunted house this year?" Hannah inquired in August, even though the Halloween festival was two months away.

"Can Linda's group get some boxes to make snail houses again this year?" Arabella asked.

"Why was cow poop on the school supply list?" Josh asked, eliciting snickers from the student body, which totaled fewer than sixty-five for grades kindergarten through fifth.

"That's for the garden. We call it manure," Marie answered very matter-of-factly. She smiled and laughed a lot, but always talked to the kids like they were on her same level. To foster this sense of mutual respect, students called teachers and classmates' parents by their first names. I still have no clue of Candace's last name, even though she taught both my daughters. The school had only four teachers and four classes, excuse me, "groups" which were made up of kids of different ages with similar academic abilities.

They learned Spanish from Nidia, a native speaker, and received music instruction from Daryl, a classmate's dad who played the guitar while the students sang "Blowin' in the Wind," "Octopus's Garden," and "Where Have All the Flowers Gone." Math in the early years consisted of counting colored stones called mermaid tears or measuring ingredients for baking cookies, while the older kids played multiplication bingo and blackjack. English also varied by age, though all students journaled every day with the youngest students drawing a picture until it was their turn to dictate one-on-one to their teacher or a parent volunteer. The first thing I'd grab if my house caught fire would be my daughters' ten or so assorted spiral journals.

Science was often taught outside by planting seeds in the garden or dissecting a dead sea cucumber that washed up on the beach. I started rolling my eyes a little at Sunflower's relaxed approach to curriculum during the spring of Olivia's first year when she came home four days in a row, reporting she'd spent hours sitting outside watching a chrysalis encasing a butterfly-to-be. Couldn't she be learning to read two-syllable words or count past fifty?

I walked through the parking lot to pick Olivia up on day five of the watch party (because car line is way too impersonal, of course), and she broke away from a group of kids to race toward me across the asphalt. "The butterfly emerged from the chrysalis, and we saw it fly away," she yelled. "Come see the empty chrysalis."

I can still picture her dirty blond curls, dirty bare feet, and wide blue eyes as she told me. I don't remember a single thing about the day she counted past fifty.

"Oh, Sunflower. Isn't that the school where they learn when they want to?" a neighbor commented when we moved Olivia there. It was a catty comment that was actually true and turned out not to be a bad thing. By the end of first grade, several of Olivia's classmates at her original school were getting tutored over the summer because they weren't reading on grade level while Olivia was consuming children's versions of all the classics, like *Moby Dick* and *Tom Sawyer*. My mother gave her *Shakespeare's Stories for Young Readers*, and she took it everywhere. Her love for the bard sprouted from Sunflower's annual Shakespeare play put on by the third-, fourth-, and fifth-graders.

Marie and Candace condensed the plays so they ran about two hours, but they were still in Shakespeare's exact words. The students spent six weeks learning lines, painting sets, and getting fitted for costumes made from thrift store evening gowns. They practiced jousting with Styrofoam swords, made bloody and bedazzled knives and goblets, and painted portraits of their characters. Olivia's roles included Hippolyta from *A Midsummer Night's Dream*, Casca from *Julius Caesar*, and Viola from *Twelfth Night*. Charlotte was the soothsayer in *Julius Caesar*, Caliban in *The Tempest,* and Juliet.

Both my daughters struggle to tell time on an ordinal clock, and they can barely decipher cursive. But they blossomed at Sunflower, Olivia because she was allowed to let her creativity fly and Charlotte, our quiet one, gained confidence and emerged a strong leader with a love of off-beat music and art.

The standing ovations they got playing Viola and Juliet didn't hurt either.

10. No Autographs Please

My parents and I arrived at the bridge of the *Queen Mary 2* at the appointed time to watch the captain maneuver the 1,100-foot-long ship out of a small boat slip in Cancun, Mexico.

We were invited to this VIP experience because my dad called the ship's public relations people with a few questions before we set sail. He was writing a column on the six-day cruise the three of us were taking. Before the captain's show of maritime prowess began, his assistant told us we were waiting on two special guests who would be joining us.

What? There were passengers onboard the *QM2* with more VIP status than a columnist for the Raleigh *News & Observer*?

Within a few minutes, in walked acclaimed actress Angela Bassett and her husband, Courtney Vance. I loved her in *What's Love Got to Do with It* and had watched *Akeelah and the Bee* at least ten times with my kids, and five more times alone. I also felt a special connection to the actress because she grew up in St. Petersburg, where I lived at the time.

As introductions were made, I shook Bassett's hand vigorously and announced: "Guess what? I live in St. Petersburg, Florida."

She smiled politely but said nothing to acknowledge her hometown. To the captain of the *QM2*, Bassett's husband, and the rest of the crowd who were thinking I was an idiot, I might as well have said: "I live in Topeka, Kansas," or "I'm from Mars," or "I brush after every meal."

I felt the heat from my red face and silently cursed myself for being too pushy as the captain steered the ship out of the narrow slip with such effortless precision that my father would later describe it in his column as "like he was backing a small Volkswagen out of a generous parking space at the Harris Teeter."

My embarrassment was payment for breaking the rule all non-famous people somehow learn early: Don't bother the famous in private situations. They give on stage, they give on screen, don't ask them to give 24-7, no matter how much money they make.

I learned this rule doesn't apply only to rubes south of the Mason-Dixon line when my former mother-in-law chastised me for requesting tickets from her friend Hal Gurnee, director of both of David Letterman's talk shows. Even though my ask was on behalf of the local Children's Dream Fund, which was sending a sick teenager to New York City, it didn't matter.

"Katherine! We are not star-fuckers. We do not ask famous people for favors," she told me.

I haven't requested any free stuff from anyone since, but I admit I am still way too infatuated with famous people. I actually added a "Celebrity Corner" component to my frequent phone conversations with my friend Beth, who lives in Raleigh.

I got the idea from one of my favorite writers, David Sedaris, who is quite famous himself, having written more than a dozen books translated into twenty-seven languages.

But before he was a celebrity in his own right, Sedaris taught a writing class in Chicago shortly after graduating college. He added Celebrity Corner to his curriculum, so he'd have less class time to fill. In the book *Me Talk Pretty One Day*, Sedaris explained that most students had friends in L.A. or New York who provided gossip about which band was about to break up or which movie stars were having secret sexual trysts.

Beth shares my shallow infatuation with anyone remotely famous or infamous, so after reading Sedaris' book, I suggested we make Celebrity Corner a standing agenda item for our frequent calls.

Reading *People* isn't enough; we like first-, second-, or seventeenth-hand knowledge of what famous people are like in real life. Sometimes we have a personal interaction to share, though usually there are multiple degrees of separation.

She spotted Anderson Cooper having brunch in London. He was very nice to the server and in extremely good shape.

I met a man in St. Petersburg whose cousin was Matt Lauer's first wife. They had a very amicable divorce when their careers took them to separate coasts. She actually made a statement in his defense during his Me-Too comeuppance. (I don't think it helped much.)

Beth's aunt was at a spa where Caroline Kennedy, Maria Shriver, and a few other Kennedy women were also staying. They had relay races in the pool and joked around a lot.

Though Angela Bassett made me feel like a fool, the encounter was still a pretty good Celebrity Corner entry because I spotted her several times throughout the rest of the cruise singing to her twins, who were toddlers at the time. I never noticed a nanny helping her out.

But soon after that, Beth had her own impressive submission. Her husband, Julian, found himself in line next to Gayle King during the 2005 NCAA Final Four in St. Louis. At the time, King was dating the father of Sean May, who played for UNC. This was when she was mostly known for being Oprah's bestie, since it was several years before she became a host of *CBS This Morning*.

Julian didn't know what to say when he saw King, but he'd never shy away from a conversation with anyone, famous or not, so he offered up: "Hey, Gayle. How's Oprah?"

"She's doing well. She said to tell you hello," King replied dryly.

Another Raleigh friend, Johnny McConnell, met Chris Rock at a mall in Indianapolis before a Colts game. Mr. McConnell is the father of my friend Elizabeth. His picture is next to "never met a stranger" in *Bartlett's Quotations*.

While they were wandering around a store, Mr. McConnell's grandson told him he'd just seen Chris Rock and pointed him out. Within seconds, Mr. McConnell was by the comedian's side offering his hand.

"Johnny McConnell, Raleigh, North Carolina. Nice to meet you, Chris."

"Chris Rock, nice to meet you," the celebrity replied.

"So, Chris, how do you know my grandson?" Johnny inquired.

After a who's-on-first conversation, Mr. McConnell realized Chris Rock wasn't an acquaintance of his grandson in the slightest but was a famous person his grandson had merely recognized. Rock got a big laugh out of it, and told Mr. McConnell he was a hell of a guy.

My parents also naively hung out with someone rich and famous. Years ago, in San Francisco, they wandered into an art gallery that was full of well-dressed patrons and waiters serving wine and cheese. They helped themselves and pondered the paintings on the wall for a while before noticing Tony Bennett standing a few feet away.

"Oh my stars, you're Tony Bennett," my mother said, in case he was suffering a bout of amnesia.

"Yes I am. I'm so glad you could make it tonight," the legendary singer said as he shook their hands.

Turns out my parents had crashed an invitation-only exhibition of Bennett's art. They were mortified, apologized, and headed for the door, but Bennett insisted they stay. He offered them another glass of wine and introduced his friends.

Bennett's picture is also in *Bartlett's Quotations*, next to "class act."

It's a feel-good moment when celebrities are revealed to be down-to-earth, or better yet, extremely kind. Knowing his acidic honesty, I didn't expect David Sedaris to be a softie. Still, after the fourth time I saw him bring thousands of people to their feet after reading his essays aloud on a stage, I stood in line to get a couple well-worn paperbacks autographed when he was at Tampa's Straz Center for the Performing Arts.

As I approached him my heart rate spiked, and I reminded myself yet again of the soundbite I'd engraved on my frontal lobe.

"We both grew up in Raleigh. Have you heard of A. C. Snow? He's written a column in the paper for about 100 years. He's my father."

Sedaris stood up. It was all I could do not to take this as a cue to bow at his feet.

"Oh my God, of course I've heard of A. C. Snow. I think about him sometimes."

"Why in the world would you ever think about A. C. Snow?" I asked.

"Because he came up with a new column every week for so many years, and they were always good," Sedaris replied. "I wonder how he kept coming up with new material."

In his book, *Naked*, he inscribed: "I'll meet you at Crabtree," referring to the mall near his childhood home and mine.

He signed *Me Talk Pretty One Day*:

"Sno' mistake. We finally meet," as a reference to my dad's column "Sno' Foolin."

I called Beth on the way home for an emergency edition of Celebrity Corner.

—◦◦◦—

11. Family Secrets Aren't Meant to Be Shared

‿⸾⸾⸽⸽

*R*each into the freezer to grab ice for your vodka tonic at any supper club across the South and if the hostess has children thirteen or younger, there's a decent chance you'll find a hairbrush next to the frozen macarons from Trader Joe's. This is because lice and their eggs are believed to die after ten to twelve hours in subzero temperatures.

It's also common these days to see Ford Fiestas with magnetic signs reading "Lice Fairy" or "Lice b' Gone" parked in long driveways shaded by tall oaks in all the best neighborhoods. When lice invaded an elite private school in Charlotte, contaminated students were required to bring in empty boxes of Rid to gain re-entry to class.

The first time I ever heard of the blood-sucking creatures was when Mammy was berated by Scarlett's sister, Suellen, for her system of decontaminating beleaguered Confederate soldiers coming home from the Civil War. Mammy made the men undress behind a makeshift wall of quilts and then hand her their uniforms, which she deposited into boiling water laced with lye soap.

"I think it's humiliating the way you're treating Mr. Kennedy," Suellen said of her beau, who would later become Scarlett's husband. "You'd be a sight more humiliated if Mr. Kennedy's lice gets on you," Mammy warned.

Today's lice are not the lice that Mammy conquered with one washing. Lice of the twenty-first century are super-atomic parasites that appear to have grown immune to chemical intervention. Private and public schools across the country are grappling with students spreading it around the sleepover and sports circuits.

Our first encounter came when my daughters were in second and fourth grades at Sunflower School. It was about 8:00 p.m. one night when I somehow spotted a translucent gray bug creeping along Olivia's dirty blond scalp. I turned to check Charlotte and there was a convoy of three bugs trucking across the part of her straight, shiny black hair.

In a panic I called Tinuviel, the parent of a Sunflower classmate, who had a last name but nobody knew it because when you are named after one of J. R. R. Tolkien's elves you don't really need a last name. As a professional hairstylist with great knowledge of how to get rid of lice, she had become the most powerful woman at school, making $50 an hour to go through our children's hair with thin wooden barbecue skewers picking out lice and their eggs. The eggs are called nits, thus the phrase. Tinuviel's fee included her unflappable aura and blatant annoyance at the other parents' panic.

"They can't hurt you," she'd say as she flicked an egg half the size of a grain of rice into a red Solo cup filled with rubbing alcohol.

"But don't you need to squish that?" I nervously asked.

"What do you think? The lice are going to hatch, swim to the side of the cup, climb up, and chase after you?" she'd laugh while my daughters shot me pleading looks to just be quiet and let the master do her work.

I laugh now, laugh at the fear I once suffered because of those pathetic little bugs. The next year, when Tinuviel and her son were living in Costa Rica, lice struck Sunflower School again. This time it was I who was wielding the barbecue skewers along with Angie, another mom who studied under Tinuviel. We perched ourselves on the picnic table in the school parking lot with students sitting between our knees on the benches. Manipulating their hair with the sticks, we divided it into razor-thin segments and looked closely from root to tip for invaders. We picked each head as clean as we could, but the kids still had to go home and show up to school free of lice the next day to gain admittance. While we didn't get paid, we felt it was our civic duty, and also our diligence helped protect our own children and homes from infestation.

Like all issues at Sunflower, lice were discussed in the daily morning meeting where students were reminded not to share hats and hairbrushes or to attach any kind of stigma to those who were infested. When a boy was sent home on a Tuesday and came in on Wednesday with a shaved head, the sea of students parted in awe to make way for him. One girl missed a week of school because, even though we picked her clean in the parking lot each morning, the bugs were still living in the little girl's house and kept reinfesting her hair. All the students made her construction paper cards with "We miss you Molly" and "lice are not nice" scrawled in Crayola. Nobody, students or parents, raised an eyebrow at the red Solo cups brimming with nits floating in rubbing alcohol or the nitpickers lined up on the picnic table next to the school's entrance, because getting lice was seen as nothing different from catching a cold.

When my daughter Charlotte was transitioning to Lutheran Church of the Cross's middle school, however, she didn't feel as comfortable comparing notes and nits with her classmates. Yes, lice of the twenty-first century aren't just for elementary kids rolling around on Dora the Explorer rugs. Thanks to travel soccer and competitive cheerleading teams, older kids who contract lice from younger siblings pass them along as easily as they share

Snapchat stories. Lice have joined pimples and periods as yet another middle school rite of passage.

Though Charlotte wasn't infested, many of her friends were sent home from school with the critters and a note saying they could return once they used some Rid. (The Lutherans, apparently more trusting than that nondenominational school in Charlotte, required no proof of purchase.)

"Rid doesn't work unless you do it exactly right and still pick out every nit after you wash the hair," I bemoaned to Charlotte when she came home reporting that half the girls in her class now had lice. "Somebody needs to check every single head before they come back to school."

"Mom! Don't. Please do not go to LCC and pick lice," Charlotte begged. "This isn't Sunflower."

"You'd be a sight more humiliated if LCC's lice gets on you," I said.

She had no idea what I meant, but I knew what she meant. Because LCC Day School went from pre-kindergarten to eighth grade, Charlotte coming in at sixth grade was the new girl during the most angst-ridden phase of education. Even the veterans who had been together since they were transitioning from Pull-Ups to Cinderella underwear were now sizing up each other differently.

Charlotte found a group of girls who welcomed her at their lunch table and texted her with homework questions and LOLs. One girl even felt close enough to warn her that the group's aspiring queen bee complained: "Has anyone noticed how Charlotte used to kind of walk behind us and now she walks beside us?" Though the comment hurt, Charlotte felt camaraderie with the source and could sense she was being accepted by girls who appreciated her quiet ways, easy smile, and smart contributions in class, so I kept barbecue skewers in remission as long as I could.

A week later, however, Charlotte had lice. I told her I was calling the school's director just to explain what I knew but would not offer to check heads.

"I don't have many talents, but I do know a little bit about lice. The best way to get rid of them is not with that special shampoo but by picking out the nits," I told Mrs. Stroud over the phone.

"Thank you so much for calling. Is there any way you can show us exactly what to do?" she asked.

Before I knew it, I was on the patio outside the middle school office with the school secretary and P.E. teacher showing them how to discern a nit from dandruff. I assured my proteges that dropping the lice and nits into a cup of rubbing alcohol would kill them. There was no need to squish the eggs. It's not like they were going to hatch and crawl up the side of the cup and then chase after them.

We set up a line in the sand that students had to cross before they could return to school and gave them the numbers of the Lice Fairy and other nitpickers for hire. Charlotte was mortified, but after my second day on lice patrol her new friends' moms started calling.

"I heard you have been helping with the lice. Thank you so much. Is there any chance you could look at my head?" one said to me. "And we just adore Charlotte. Can she go out on the boat with us this weekend?"

"My husband's head has been itching since this whole thing started. I have no idea what I'm looking for," another said. "This is so much to ask, but could he stop by your house on his way home from work? And could Charlotte spend the night this weekend?"

I don't think the newfound social clout with the middle school moms was only because I carried the prestigious title of Lice Mom. Maybe one way to mesh with a new group is to admit you have their same worries and angst.

But you better believe I checked every one of those girls' heads before they spent one night in our house or Charlotte stayed with them.

12. A Minute on the Lips,

Forever on the Hips

～

Shortly after we got married, my former husband and I went to a party for new members of the church we joined. A guest urged me to try the key lime pie, and I told her I was doing Weight Watchers to shed the pounds I'd gained since the wedding.

"Oh yeah. That's what happens," her husband commented. "The bride loses all this weight for the wedding, then as soon as she says, 'I do,' it's like pulling the ripcord on a life raft."

I should have slapped him, but I was young and in my pre-bitter years. I actually laughed hard enough that I choked a little on my white wine spritzer. (Half as many Weight Watchers points as a glass of wine.)

At five feet, two inches, with a longtime commitment to Dairy Queen's Oreo-and-Butterfinger Blizzards, I have always been on some kind of diet or at least constantly aware that I shouldn't have eaten what I just ate. My first crash diet was freshman year in college when a group of us tried to lose ten pounds in five days before Spring Break on the potato diet. We ate a baked potato for breakfast, one for lunch, and one for dinner. That last one was our splurge because we melted a low-fat orange square that slightly resembled cheese on it. We lost about five pounds and gained it all back with the first slice of pizza.

The next year, I tried SlimFast for a week. "A shake for breakfast, a shake for lunch, and a sensible dinner" sounded easy enough. I quickly grew tired of the vanilla and chocolate shakes, however when I whipped them up in the blender with an Oreo or two the shakes weren't so bad. I also added Kahlua for a low-fat play on a White Russian. I gained three pounds.

Weight Watchers, which is now Wellness Works, was and still is the program that's worked best for me for several decades. I'm a card-carrying lifetime member who's been a devotee through the days of the food scale, the cardboard slide rule era, and now the smart phone app that scans barcodes to calculate points. I've signed up and dropped out of Weight Watchers at least ten times in the past thirty years, racking up more than a hundred meetings in strip malls, church basements, and even the conference room at the *Tampa Bay Times* for the Lose-It-At-Work program.

I was there when vegetables became points-free and a few years later when lean chicken and boiled eggs were declared free as well. After that global shift, a woman at a meeting told Anthony, our hilariously honest group leader, she was worried she would end up eating too many hard-boiled eggs.

"Honey, I don't think any of us got here from eating too many hard-boiled eggs," he answered. The best leaders have a sense of humor and a doctorate in psychology. Women share tearful tales of husbands who still insist on chicken-fried steak and deep-dish chocolate pie while red-faced men tell of friends who tease them for declining nachos at the game. Some members talk on and on and on about anything from the chocolate buffet on a cruise to Cancun they took seven years ago to the great deals they get on wine at the Aldi on 34th Street South. They just want to talk. The heroic leaders know how to comfort members who see Weight Watchers as group therapy, yet still keep meetings on track and dole out helpful advice.

After I turned fifty, I gave a couple lackluster tries at Weight Watchers but didn't really commit to counting points and going to meetings. (Going to meetings is how I ultimately lose the weight.)

One of the twenty-somethings at the public relations firm where I was working was doing this intermittent fasting thing, eating only eight hours a day from noon to 8:00 p.m.

I gave it a try and by 9:15 a.m. the first day I saw a mirage of a baked potato. On the third day, I had to fast anyway for blood-work at the lab. As the technician was drawing my blood at 8:30 a.m. she asked what I was planning to eat as soon as she was done.

"This is ridiculous, but I'm not eating until noon. I'm doing this intermittent fasting thing with my friend at work," I answered.

"What's your friend's name?" she asked.

"Alana," I said.

"Well, let me tell you something. Alana is crazy. Alana has lost her mind."

"Well, she says I'll get used to it."

"What did I just say? Alana has lost her mind. That girl doesn't even know what she's saying."

"You may be right."

"I know I'm right. Don't listen to Alana. That's no way to live. You and Alana need to stop that nonsense."

This conversation was my hall pass to give up on intermittent fasting, but six months later, I signed up for something even more out of my league called Faster Way to Fat Loss. It's based not only on intermittent fasting but also prescribed workouts and a rotation of high-carb days, high-fat days, low-carb days, and low-fat days. My local leader was low pressure and very helpful. She made great food suggestions including using Trader Joe's rosemary chicken to make chicken salad with mayonnaise for the high fat days. I had not eaten mayonnaise since 1984 because of all the fat, so I was excited to try it again. I checked the nutrition label and learned one cup has ten grams of fat, so I mixed two cups with four chicken breasts to boost my fat intake. I didn't remember chicken salad being so much like mayonnaise soup but forced it down and waited for the pounds to melt off of me.

I told a friend about the diet and my high-fat chicken salad.

"Katherine, that's not right. You never put that much mayonnaise in chicken salad unless you're feeding like thirty people," she said. We went and checked the nutrition label on the mayonnaise in her refrigerator and found that it's one *tablespoon*, not one *cup*, that has ten grams of fat. A cup of mayonnaise has 160 grams of fat. Two cups, have 320. Gross.

I didn't give up, however, because I was feeling stronger from the prescribed daily workouts and knew I could figure out the food. On the next high-fat day, by the time I left work I was way behind on my fat intake and had thirty minutes left before I was done eating for the day.

I pulled into Trader Joe's, bought two avocados, hopped back in my car, peeled them with the aid of a ball point pen and my fingers, and ate each one like an apple. I arrived at a friend's birthday gathering with avocado caked beneath my fingernails and a racing heart.

"Katherine, this diet is stressing me out, and I'm not even on it," Biz said, offering me a glass of wine. I broke the Faster Way to Fat Loss rules and had a glass of Chalk Hill past the 8:00 p.m. cutoff.

After another week, I told my Faster Way coach that I loved the prescribed workouts and was finally doing weights instead of just cardio, but the food regimen was too time consuming and stressful for me. She assured me it takes time to get used to it, and I was doing well. She asked if I was watching the Facebook videos that were posted a few times a week and said they would really help me stay on track.

"I just haven't had time. I thought I'd watch them all this weekend," I confessed.

"Try watching them in the morning when you are putting on your makeup. Just prop your phone up on your makeup table," she advised.

"Oh, that's a good idea," I lied. I put my makeup on at stoplights.

This was my cue to give up on Faster Way to Fat Loss. As with many things in life, the same approach doesn't work for everyone. We just do the best we can to be healthy and try not to judge anyone who slips Oreos into their SlimFast.

13. Your Children Always Come First

 ❧

The pediatrician studied the glob of pus oozing from the patch-work of scabs along my one-year-old son's left index finger. "It's definitely infected. And you have no idea when or how it happened?" he asked.

"I could charge you with gross negligence of your third child and subject you to a court of your peers who would most certainly revoke that Mother's Day card with two little handprints this sweet boy made for you before your failed attempt at mother-hood led to the maiming of one of those hands," he added. Well, he didn't say those exact words, but that's pretty much what his look conveyed.

Yet again, my son Wade had been lost in the shuffle of rais-ing three kids under eight, working part-time, trying to make sure everyone had diapers and clean underwear and low-sugar jelly without aspartame and a not-too-scary costume for the

Halloween carnival, and that we were home from the dentist in time to meet the exterminator who promised to kill the rat living behind the kitchen wall before Delbert, our basset hound, bit it and caught rabies.

"I guess I didn't even hear Wade cry when he cut his finger on a knife or pinched it in the pantry door," I lamented to my father on the phone that night. "Or maybe I did hear him cry and I just handed him a sippy cup and stuck him in front of *Curious George* without even noticing his finger was bleeding."

My two older kids got nature walks, music classes, and dictated stories to me that I wrote and they illustrated, I told my dad. Wade just got dragged along for the ride our busy lives demanded.

"Good Lord, Katherine," he said. "I spent the first six months of my life in a wooden cradle in the kitchen. Your Aunt Zetta tied a string to it and ran it through the window out to the yard so she could play outside and give that string a tug to rock the cradle if I cried," he said. "My mother never read a book to me in my life, much less wrote a story for me, and I was Phi Beta Kappa at Carolina."

Daddy was the youngest of fifteen children, born to Bird and Ida Victoria Snow on a tobacco farm in western North Carolina. He could always bring life into perspective with childhood stories. His siblings said he was spoiled because he was the only one who got jelly on his biscuit. Christmas morning brought only stockings with oranges and peppermint sticks, but the Snow children were thrilled to insert the candy in the middle of the fruit and use it as a straw for sucking the fruit's sweet juice. Though the family of eleven boys and four girls lived six hours from the North Carolina coast, the first ocean my dad ever saw was the Pacific, as he crossed it in a troop carrier on his way to the Philippines during World War II.

His family lived comfortably enough until the Great Depression, and then my grandfather lost his store and the price of tobacco plummeted to seven cents a pound. There were never more than eight offspring in the house at one time, since many of the older kids were married with families of their own by the time the younger siblings were born, but my grandmother still had no time to be a doting mother. My father was born when she was forty-four, and his dad was sixty-four, so nobody was reading to him at bedtime or quizzing him on multiplication at the breakfast table. Ida didn't march into the school to complain when my dad's second-grade teacher made him wear a dunce hat and sit in the corner after his undiagnosed color blindness caused him to color the grass blue and the sky green. When a note came home saying one of his older brothers talked back to a teacher, she didn't ask her son for his side of the story. She simply told him to go to the yard and pick a branch off a tree.

"And if you come back with one that's too short, I'll pick another switch myself and your whipping will be much worse," she'd warn. Ida had to be tough because Bird (who family lore says was a softy) left all the child rearing to her.

She believed in natural consequences, too. My Uncle Warren learned that one summer when he snuck into the woods at the edge of the tobacco field to doze while the rest of the family labored in their cash crop. When the workday ended, everyone went into the house to a table sagging with Ida's country ham, sliced tomatoes, green beans, and buttermilk biscuits. Then they retired to the front room to listen to the radio and finally went to bed. Twelve-year-old Warren woke up in the woods just before 10:00 p.m. and ran almost a mile to the house, which was locked up tight. He knew better than to wake his parents and slept on the porch.

"I never snuck away from the field again," he told me once. "Mamma didn't mess around."

Of all our father's childhood stories, my sister, Melinda, and I loved the story of the ice cream truck the most. The driver, who was going way too fast for the plank bridge that crossed the creek below the Snow farm, lost control and went right into the water.

My father and his siblings, nieces, and nephews raced to the creek when they heard the crash and thought they had entered an alternate universe. The driver, unhurt but cursing up a storm, stood in two feet of water surrounded by at least a hundred drums of ice cream that had rolled out the back of the truck when the doors flew open on impact.

"Have it. Just have all of it," he angrily urged the crowd of kids. "It's all gonna melt before we get another truck in here." There were so many more flavors than the vanilla, strawberry, and chocolate that Bird had sold at the store. My dad ate almost a full gallon of pistachio by himself. Ida, who didn't tell them no, enjoyed chocolate chip.

The story that always made my sister and me cry was the one my father said meant the most to him.

When he was eight years old, he spent Christmas Eve with his oldest brother, Winfield, because Daddy was best friends with Winfield's daughter Cecil. She was his niece though she was a year older. When the sun broke on Christmas morning, Winfield's children rushed into the living room to find their stockings filled with candy and apples and a few presents wrapped in red paper, but there wasn't a thing for my dad.

"Santa Claus didn't know you were sleeping here so he left presents at your own house," Winfield explained to his disappointed youngest brother. By the time they showed up at the five-bedroom farmhouse it was close to noon and more than thirty family members were already there. The men and boys talked on the wide front porch in the unseasonably warm December weather while the women and girls worked in the kitchen under Ida's direction. My dad rushed to the living room where no stocking hung by the fireplace and no presents awaited him under the tree.

"Did Santa come for me?" he asked his mom in the midst of the crowded kitchen. She paused for a quick second and then sank into a ladder-back chair at the kitchen table.

"Didn't he leave you something at Winfield's?" she asked.

"No. Winfield said he'd come here."

Ida, who already had silver hair by age fifty-two, took my father in her arms and hugged him tightly as tears streamed down her tan face. He had never seen her cry before. It was at that moment he realized the myth of Santa Claus was truly a myth, but he also marked that Christmas as the day he knew how much his mother loved him.

Almost two decades later, after four sons and four grandsons had gone to World War II and returned unscathed, Ida Victoria went to the beauty shop for the first time and bought a suit made of pale blue silk spotted with white dogwood blossoms. Aunt Zetta drove her to Chapel Hill, and she watched her youngest son become the first college graduate in the family.

A few years ago, my former husband and I were at a supper club down the street, lingering until almost midnight as we waited for an April rainstorm to pass before walking home. I received a text from my son Wade:

"going to go to sleep now. all packed. can we go by the bank on the way to the airport tomorrow so I can get my spending money?"

I jumped out of my seat and asked our host to drive us home.

"I totally forgot Wade is going on the eighth-grade class trip to Washington, D.C., tomorrow, and we have to leave for the airport at 5:00 a.m."

The women around the table let out collective gasps.

"Oh no, Katherine," my friend Hope said. "Have you packed his suitcase?"

"No. I've done nothing. Mom-of-the-Year here. I thought about it on Friday, but we had all weekend and then I totally forgot."

We got home in less than five minutes, and I tiptoed into Wade's room.

"Hey. I haven't helped you pack. I'd rather do it now than in the morning, so I'm going to have to turn on the light. I'm so sorry."

"Why are you sorry? I packed myself. It's not a big deal," he said sleepily. "But if you want to feel less guilty you can scratch my back."

I scratched with one hand and went through his suitcase with the other. He had everything he needed, even the blazer and loafers for one formal dinner and a play.

Ida would have been proud of her youngest great-grandson.

—✺—

14. Ice, Elevate, and Stay Off of It

_P_erhaps I left my suitcase in the bathroom at Tampa International Airport on the way to Barack Obama's 2009 inauguration, because I was so journey proud.

My parents' longtime friend Sally O'Keefe introduced us to the phrase "journey proud" in the 1960s. Her husband was my dad's editor at the _Raleigh Times_, and they all traveled together from time to time.

"I'm just so journey proud I couldn't sleep last night," Sally would say when they headed off to a newspaper convention at the Blockade Runner in Wilmington, the Carolina Hotel in Pinehurst, or the Sheraton in Washington, D.C. We adopted the phrase and used it whenever we were excited and a little overwhelmed about impending travel.

Decades later, I'd hear a friend from Charlotte and another from Greenville, Alabama, talk about being journey proud and realized that it wasn't just Sally O'Keefe's term, but an actual col-loquialism. An online reference defines journey proud as "being greatly excited about a journey."

If ever there was a time to be journey proud, it was when I was sitting on a plane about to take off for Washington, D.C., to see the inauguration of our first African American president.

I was traveling solo for the first time in a while. Adam, my husband at the time and the *Tampa Bay Times* political editor, was already in our nation's capital covering the impending transition of power and a babysitter was home with our three children. I headed out with just my overstuffed carry-on suitcase, a *Vanity Fair*, and me. When the flight attendant asked passengers to make sure bags were securely stowed under the seat in front of us or in the overhead storage bin, I wanted to throw up. I immediately realized I had no bag to stow because I'd left it in the airport bathroom.

"Can you hold the plane while I run and get it?" I asked the flight attendant.

"We have to close the door in three minutes. We won't wait."

"But I'm checked in. I'm standing here telling you I'll be right back."

"We can't wait for you. I'm sorry. It's up to you if you want to deplane."

I had no time go all Ben-Stiller-from-*Meet-the-Parents* on her and made a split-second decision to go for it. I bolted off the plane, ran past six gates to the bathroom, and there sat my olive-green bag right where I'd left it outside the last stall on the right.

I grabbed it and raced back to the gate in my gray suede wedge-heel boots, picking up speed as I ran down the bridge to the plane. Too much speed, apparently. I totally busted and dragged the suitcase over my left foot as I fell.

A flight attendant came rushing out and helped me hobble onto the plane. He stowed my bag for me while I took the last seat available in the middle of the third row, reassuring alarmed passengers who had heard my tumble that I was okay and not drunk.

Flight attendants cajoled me with bags of ice, insurance waivers, and incident reports to sign throughout the flight.

I was in so much pain when I landed that I had to stop every few feet and sit down. But I soldiered on, got through the airport, and took a cab to my friend Margaret's house in Chevy Chase, Maryland.

"Katherine! Look at it," she said when I peeled off my sock to reveal a giant purple, prize-winning eggplant at the state fair. "Wait. Don't look at it," she added.

I spent the afternoon lying on Margaret's living room sofa, talking, laughing, and drinking wine with my foot encased in bags of frozen vegetables. "Time to rotate the crop," she'd say when the bags of edamame started to thaw and were replaced with frozen peas.

By late afternoon, I was sure my foot was much better because it barely hurt anymore, but when I tried to walk on it, it couldn't bear my weight. I leaned against Margaret and we made it to her car so she could drive me down the road to another friend's home where Adam and I were spending the night.

Margaret helped me limp into the house and told our hosts, Joe and Laura, that she was coming inside just long enough for the unveiling.

"Unveiling of what?" Adam asked.

"Of this," I said, pulling my pant leg up so they could see what used to be my ankle and foot.

"Oh my God," Laura gasped, leaning down to look closer and then turning her head in horror.

"What happened?" Joe asked.

"You can't go to the inauguration with that," Adam declared. "You're going to be walking all day."

"It's not like I'm *in* the parade. I'll be fine," I said as I took another dose of Advil.

I spent the rest of the evening chugging ibuprofen and elevating and icing my injury. Sally the bull terrier was allowed on the sofa for the first time in her life so she could lie next to me for comfort and also to act as a shield, hiding the purple, black, and teal hues of my foot from view.

When the alarm went off the next morning at 4:00 a.m., it was an inauguration miracle. I could distinguish my foot from my ankle. Yellow had joined the rainbow of pain, but the swelling was down. I managed to get my Nike on even though I couldn't lace it.

"Are you sure about this?" Adam asked. "It's going to be a ton of walking."

I was sure.

Even that early in the morning, the Metro was filled with excited people of all ages and races, forming a rainbow as multi-hued as my left foot.

Adam had a press pass to the seating right in front of the inaugural stage, and I had a ticket from a friend who works on the Hill. It got me passage into the so-called Purple Section, about halfway down the National Mall. The directions on my purple ticket instructed me to line up in a tunnel near the intersection of 3rd Street and C Street. All I had to do was wait a couple of hours for the gates to open, and I'd watch history in the making.

Turns out I made a little history myself along with an estimated 1,000 to 4,000 people who were stuck in what became known as the "Purple Tunnel of Doom" in the media, by the Joint Congressional Committee on Inaugural Ceremonies, and on Wikipedia. Thousands of us, including the mayor of Seattle and Kathleen Kennedy Townsend's daughters, were led into the 3rd Street Tunnel but not let out in time to get into the inauguration.

Earlier that morning, however, we all felt so lucky to possess Purple Tickets and there were no strangers in the Purple Tunnel. We were all journey proud, talking about how far we'd come, how cold it was, and how the freezing temperatures didn't dampen our excitement. After a while it seemed like the line wasn't moving, but a church choir from Georgia led my section of the dark tunnel in a singalong of "This Little Light of Mine" to help us to pass the time.

Then we started getting calls and texts from friends who were already on the National Mall, gazing at the spot where Obama would soon take the oath.

Adam sent me a picture of the Tuskegee Airmen who were sitting three rows in front of him. I sent him a picture of the cold, dark 3rd Street Tunnel full of huddled masses. He sent me a selfie with Denzel Washington. I sent him a picture of my left foot.

Finally, word spread through the inhabitants of the Purple Tunnel that we weren't moving. We'd been left in a tunnel and nobody had come back to let us proceed to the gates of the mall.

There was crying, yelling, cursing, head shaking, and disbelief.

When we finally reached the streets of D.C., we merged into a mosh pit of hundreds of other people without tickets, crowding their way to any gate of any color. Outstretched arms clutching useless purple tickets were ignored. The gates were blocked because the mall was at capacity.

As the inauguration started, I nudged my way into a group of six or so people crowding around a young woman with a handheld television. I saw my first glimpse of the almost-president and his wife, Michelle, and caught my breath. They were there. This was really happening. The cluster of strangers watched civil rights activist Joseph Lowery lead a prayer. The African American woman holding the TV cried.

When Yo-Yo Ma started playing, I got my mojo back and decided to try to get inside the gates of the National Mall. I pushed my way to the front of the crowd and told a policeman that I'd been separated from my kids somehow, flashed my purple ticket, and begged to go in and find them. He didn't really let me in, but he didn't stop me when I crawled under the wooden barricade.

I squirmed my way farther into the crowd until I reached a spot where I could maneuver a view of the Jumbotron in the distance and thus barely see the swearing in.

So, I was there with my purple foot and my purple ticket, and I saw a black man named Barack Hussein Obama become the 44th president of the United States. After crying and hugging strangers all around me, I limped back to the Metro and made my way to Joe's and Laura's house where they had watched the whole thing with friends from the comfort of their home. During a chili dinner on their long, wooden farm table, another houseguest who had come from London mentioned offhandedly he was too tired to use his two tickets to the Creative Coalition Ball, hosted by the Hollywood crowd.

"I can't believe you're not going," I said. "Sting is performing."

"So is Elvis Costello. But I have to be on a flight back at 7:00 a.m. I'm can't do it. Do you want the tickets?"

I beamed, and then remembered I had no right to take the tickets over our hosts.

"No. Joe and Laura, you two should go," I said with the same lack of sincerity as when I suggest someone at the grocery store with five items get in front of me when I have twenty and I'm already late for the school carline.

"I have to work tomorrow. I think you and Laura should go," urged Joe, the best man who ever walked the Earth.

Within twenty minutes, Laura and I were on the Metro headed back downtown. We couldn't stop laughing at ourselves going out in the frigid air at almost 10:00 p.m. to a party where we wouldn't know a soul.

I hadn't thought to pack clothes for an inaugural ball, so I'd borrowed a black silk skirt, a black top, and long, black suede boots from Laura, who is six inches taller than I am and three shoe sizes bigger. This wasn't all bad, since my left foot was quite swollen again after I walked seventy-seven miles that day.

We made our entrance at the Harman Center for the Arts just as the entertainment portion of the evening was starting. Celebrity hosts including Susan Sarandon, Kerry Washington, Anne Hathaway, and Spike Lee gathered on the stage of the 755-seat theater.

Matthew Modine introduced Elvis Costello and thanked him for the song "Alison" because it really got his high school girlfriend of the same name in the mood back in the day.

Elvis Costello pointed out he wasn't even a registered U.S. voter but his wife, Diana Krall, was Canadian, so that must count for something. Then he belted out "Alison," "Watching the Detectives," and a few other classics.

Sting came on next and said he also wasn't registered to vote in America but was still thrilled as hell with the new president. He modified the lyrics of "Message in a Bottle" and had the audience repeatedly chant, "O-bam-a heard our message in a bottle."

After the concert, Laura and I went upstairs to get a drink and passed Ron Howard on his way down.

I'd loved the guy ever since I'd grown up watching reruns of *The Andy Griffith Show* three times a day, which is required of all elementary students in the state of North Carolina. He became an extra-favorite celebrity when he paired up with past co-stars Andy Griffith and Henry Winkler on a "Funny or Die" video for the Obama campaign. Howard went barefoot and toted a fishing rod to once again portray Opie Taylor asking his pa Andy why people were so afraid of change. Andy offered simple but wise words as always. Howard then donned his Jefferson High letterman jacket to encourage Fonzie to embrace change.

I must have gasped, stared, or looked like an all-around starstruck stalker as we rubbed elbows on the stairs. In hindsight, it might have been more of an elbow grab than a rub; I don't recall the details. The major detail, however, is Ron Howard stopped, looked straight at me, and said, "Hey. How are you?"

"I'm great. What a great day," I blurted out. He agreed and I blathered on:

"I'm from North Carolina. My dad grew up in the same town that Andy Griffith is from. The one Mayberry is based on. It's called Mount Airy. He actually grew up in Dobson, which is even smaller than Mount Airy, but it's all right there together."

"Oh, yeah," Howard said. "I know all about Mount Airy."

"I loved what you did in the video with Andy for Obama."

"It was great to work with him again. Thanks a lot," he said so sincerely and appreciatively that I think he really did need my approval to feel whole.

Then he quickly moved on down the stairs to the people who would congratulate him on *Frost/Nixon*, the movie he had just directed and that was the talk of Hollywood and Washington. Not me. I was all about a role from forty years back.

Laura and I flitted about the party stargazing and celebrating a few hours longer before making it back home around 3:00 a.m. I'd been awake and mostly out and about for twenty-three hours straight. If only I hadn't had a bum foot, I'd have made it to twenty-four.

—✕✕✕—

NANTUCKET, MASS.

15. Don't Move Without a Job

My parents stood beside a plate-glass window at the Raleigh-Durham Airport, waving goodbye to my Boston-bound plane.

"That's the last you'll ever see of that money," my father said to my mother, she told me later. "Katherine has a very short future in any of the jobs she's mentioned she might get. Housekeeping? She hardly makes her own bed. Waitressing? Can't put her plate in the dishwasher without spilling crumbs. Working a cash register? She's terrible at math."

My mother had loaned me $1,000 to pay my share of a summer rental in Nantucket, where eleven friends and I planned to live and work the summer after our sophomore year at Carolina.

I paid her back in full by July 10, thank you very much.

With no waitressing experience, I fibbed my way into a job at one of the finest restaurants on the island, and by July 4, I was making $100 in cash five nights a week. Never mind that I couldn't memorize the eight or more nightly specials, and we weren't allowed to read notes off the back of our order pad like I'd seen the waitresses do at Bennigan's. When guests asked me at 6:00 p.m. what delectable meal the people at the next table were enjoying, I had no idea. So, I'd apologize that we were already out of that special, even though the restaurant had only been open thirty minutes.

Two of my friends drove up to Nantucket first and found a three-bedroom house owned by a lawyer who presented them with an iron-clad rental contract that stated seven times in English, five times in Japanese, and twice in a strong Boston brogue that no more than six people could stay in the house at any point. No guests allowed.

So, six of us signed our twenty-year-old lives away, and we moved twelve girls into the two-story shingled house on Back Street. After our first keg party, we were known among the summer college crowd and Nantucket police as the Back Street Girls.

We divided into rooms, set up a rotation schedule for who slept on the floor and who had a bed, and embraced the first time we'd lived and worked on our own.

Since Southern schools got out earlier than our counterparts to the north, we had first crack at jobs, but before Memorial Day nobody was hiring except the Finast grocery store. Two housemates and I scored positions as cashiers, but my dad's prediction was right. Too much math, plus there was a language barrier we hadn't expected.

One afternoon our manager, Mary, asked us to go outside to collect all the cots and bring them inside. We brought in all the beach chairs, laughing amongst ourselves that she called them cots.

"What the hell is this?" Mary asked when she saw a dozen folding lounge chairs arranged in a neat row at the end of Aisle 2.

"You told us to bring in the cots," I offered up meekly to the Great and Powerful Mary.

"That's right. Cots. Not lounge chairs."

The store's assistant manager acted as an interpreter, and we realized Mary wanted us to bring in the *carts*, not the *cots*. My friends and I laughed. Mary didn't find what was lost in translation quite as amusing and warned us we had just one more chance.

We spent the next three nights studying the Finast's universal Price Look-Up codes to sharpen our recall of what numbers went with which items. Regularly purchased items were assigned three numbers that we keyed into the cash register so that each loaf of Portuguese bread or box of spaghetti didn't have to have its own price tag. Bananas were 243, apples 256, Lay's plain potato chips 125. Soon I knew the PLU codes better than my multiplication tables.

Still, the numbers proved to be too much for me. When I transposed the PLU for Breyers ice cream, 228, with cat food, 282, and greatly overcharged a customer buying sixty cans of seafood-flavored morsels, I was fired.

Within a week my friends were sacked, too. But not before Kevin Dobson, heartthrob of *Knot's Landing*, came through their line buying a pack of Gillette razors. PLU 222.

I ended up at the Ropewalk restaurant right on the water, and they got jobs as housekeepers at the Cliffside Inn. Other Back Street Girls worked at Provisions sandwich shop, Young's Bicycle Shop, Cumberland Farms, and the Juice Bar, which sold the best ice cream in New England and very little juice.

By July we had settled into a routine of alternating between beds and the floor for sleep, Cisco and Madaket for beach days, and The Chicken Box and The Muse for nights out.

Two roommates and I went off island one weekend to New York City to visit our UNC friend Whitney, who was taking summer classes at Parsons School of Design. She planned our weekend, and despite her best efforts, it was a late '80s rendition of Country Mice Come to Town.

—※—

To reach New York City, we took a ferry, bus, plane, and another bus from Newark to Grand Central Station. After an exhausting day of travel, we were thrilled that a nice man with the cab company met us with an umbrella the moment we stepped from the bus onto the Big Apple pavement. He asked where we were going and calculated it would cost $20 a person for his partner driving the cab to get us to our hotel.

"This is soooo easy," I said to my friends, as he shepherded us to the cab. When we arrived at the Sheraton Midtown our cab driver informed us we owed him $18 total for the fare. Believe it or not, he had no idea who that man was who hailed his cab. We were taken for $60 before spending even sixty seconds in New York.

The next two days were spent at Central Park and SoHo, all of us rubbernecking in hopes of spotting a celebrity to no avail. Finally, we could consider the weekend a success after we spotted a tall, dark man leaving a Vidal Sassoon salon almost a block away and declared him the man himself. Vidal Sassoon popularized the angular haircut and turned high-end hair products into a retail offering for the masses, and we saw him in the flesh.

Was he just a handsome man exiting the salon and not Vidal himself? Did Vidal really go to all his namesake salons? We pondered these questions but all agreed it was definitely the man, the myth, the legend himself.

At *M. Butterfly,* we were the only people on Broadway who didn't know the plot. When the beautiful opera singer stripped down to nothing, we were more surprised than her lover of ten years to realize that she was a he.

After wrapping our minds around that one, we met up with a couple friends from Carolina who were working in New York for the summer. When we had a few beers at their tiny apartment across from the studio where they filmed *All My Children*, Vidal Sassoon became a distant memory.

Right outside the studio was a sign reading "Pine Valley. Where Anything Can Happen." We spent the evening with eyes glued across the street and are certain we saw Susan Lucci leaving after a long day at work.

Back on Nantucket, the next weekend we threw a keg party

and all those years watching *Risky Business* paid off when our landlords called to say they were on their way over because neighbors had alerted them there was trouble on Back Street. Why they warned us, I have no idea, but there was just enough lead time for the twelve of us to push forty college kids out of the front and back doors, throw beer cans into trash bags, and load the keg and six extra roommates into a Rabbit Cabriolet headed to the beach. By the time our landlords arrived, the six legal inhabitants were playing a cutthroat game of Trivial Pursuit.

"Well, we had a few people over earlier for a cookout, but then we decided we wanted a girls' night in," I explained when they asked what happened to the party.

"The next-door neighbor said she saw a couple fornicating on our lawn," yelled the wife who co-owned the house.

"Gross, who took a dump in the yard?" one of my roommates blurted out.

We didn't get kicked out, we didn't throw any more parties, and we all learned the definition of fornicate.

Fast forward thirty years and my daughter Charlotte was eighteen, about to graduate high school, and asking to spend a gap year working at hostels and farms in Europe in exchange for free room and board. I complained to a friend, who was a Nantucket roommate all those years ago, that this plan seemed too farfetched.

"She's ridiculous. I'm just supposed to send her off with no job or place to live," I lamented.

"Didn't your parents think you going to Nantucket without a job or a place to live was ridiculous?" my roommate Kate reminded me. "But they let you go."

She was right. We let Charlotte go. But believe you me, I called Kate when Charlotte missed a ferry crossing the North Sea and had to spend the night on a bench at a deserted dock in the Netherlands waiting eight hours for the next boat.

16. Don't Talk About Death to the Dying

⌒~∽

I assumed it was a wrong number when my phone rang at 2:30 a.m. and didn't budge to answer. It rang again a minute later so I grabbed it.

"Hello?"

"Katherine?"

"Yes."

"This is Lana, Lori's sister. I am so sorry to bother you, but she's hoping you can help her write the letters."

Six months earlier, Lori Crotts and two other moms from my oldest daughter's Girl Scout troop met for dinner at a Mexican restaurant in St. Petersburg. All of our daughters except Lori's were long out of scouts, but we had remained friends after bonding over silly skits around the campfire and long talks in sunny fields at state parks while the girls worked on badges. When we met for dinner that July, Lori had colon cancer and was fighting for her life.

She assured us she was going to beat the cancer and become the poster child for the experimental drugs she was taking. We all agreed. Still, she wondered if she should write letters to her children in case she didn't make it.

"You don't need to do that," one friend assured her. "You're going to be fine."

"Absolutely," another added. "You have to think positively."

The thought of her saying parting words to three teenage children was heartbreaking and terrifying, but I didn't completely go along with all the positive thinking.

"Well, it wouldn't hurt to have some letters tucked away somewhere," I said. "I don't have many talents, but I can type pretty damn fast. If you decide to write them, call me. I promise not to cry or say anything. I'll just take dictation."

"I'll think about it," Lori said, as the others shot me sad looks. Why had I brought the possibility of death into our cheer-leading session?

Lori had just gotten back from a week in Atlanta where she'd learned to totally change her way of eating and hoped it would alter the cancer's attack on her body. But it's not like she was an unhealthy eater. I'd easily down a sleeve of graham crackers and a few Hershey bars while Lori nibbled on an apple as she lit the campfire for s'mores.

I once spent a morning planning Troop 519's pilgrimage to Savannah, the birthplace of Girl Scouts founder Juliette Gordon Low. On this particular day, Lori was also hosting her older son's high school football team for dinner so she was baking about 150 brownies. As we booked reservations online for a Southern buffet at Holden House, a tour of a church on the Underground Railroad, and a visit to Flannery O'Connor's childhood home, Lori steadily removed one pan from the oven and put another one in. She wasn't even licking the spoon, much less eating an actual finished product.

Finally, when the picture of the Savannah River transformed into the luscious dark moat from *Charlie and the Chocolate Factory* and I kept referring to Juliette Gordon Low as Betty Crocker, I broke under the pressure.

"Lori, could you possibly spare one of those 150 brownies or what?"

"Oh, my gosh, I'm so sorry," my Midwestern friend gushed. "I just never eat when I'm baking."

"Well, you see, I do. My jeans are so loose that I can button them if I lie down on the bathroom floor and hold my breath and frankly, that's just not challenging enough."

Lori was beautiful, smart, focused, and always in control. Oh yeah, she was a major runner, too. I wanted to hate her, but I just couldn't. She laughed loudly and sincerely, loved to hike, had a badass obsession with Jon Bon Jovi, and traveled the country watching him perform.

Once on a campout, she asked us fellow moms if we thought the thirteen-year-old girls would be up for a dance party in the woods.

"I don't know, Lori. I hate to extinguish your dance fever, but they might think that's a little babyish," I told her. She smartly ignored me, loaded eight fat D batteries into her vintage Panasonic boombox, and pushed play. The girls loved it and danced in the woods for more than an hour.

Beyond Girl Scouts, we weren't in each other's close circle of friends. But we had lunch once or twice a year, and Lori gave me regular book recommendations. She read constantly and suggested what are now some of my favorite books. Long before *Water for Elephants* was on everyone's bedside table, Lori was a fan. She had just finished *Wonder* a couple weeks before she was diagnosed with cancer and told me she'd consumed it faster than any book she'd ever read.

"It's hard to explain, but you would love it," she said when I ran into her at the gym. "You've got to read it."

"I'll put it on my list," I promised.

The next day a new copy of the bright blue book was on my doorstep. It was a young adult book, but the story was heavy. A boy in Brooklyn with a severely deformed face was transitioning from being homeschooled to attending a small middle school. The story highlights bravery, fear, kindness, stupidity, cowardice, insecurity, and tenacity. It took me less than a week to read it, and I saw five or more people of all ages at the gym reading the same book as they rode the stationary bike or ran on the treadmill. The bright blue copies of *Wonder*, a *New York Times* best seller, were all compliments of Lori.

Over the next couple of months after our summer dinner, the cancerous tumors didn't get bigger, but they also didn't shrink. Lori was busy checking off things on the "to do" list she'd written on the chalkboard in her kitchen. A couple more Bon Jovi concerts, hiking a mile on the Appalachian Trail with one of her sons, seeing her daughter get the Girl Scout Gold Award, and bringing an author to her book club.

The group of avid readers had talked about that for years but never made it happen. Then they did make it happen, for Lori. About fifteen women pooled their money to fly R. J. Palacio, the author of *Wonder*, from New York to St. Petersburg on a breezy day in October. Lori sat quietly beaming next to the guest of honor. I wrote a story about it for the *Tampa Bay Times* and received more than forty calls and emails from people saying the article prompted them to buy the book. Many were teachers who said they or their schools were making *Wonder* required reading.

After that call woke me in the middle of the night, I was at Lori's house in fifteen minutes.

"I told Lana you'd come," Lori whispered when I sat on the edge of her bed that night to write the letters. "I want to go outside."

Her husband and children were asleep in other rooms. Lana and I each put an arm under her arms and pretty much carried her out to the front yard. It was peaceful and pleasant in the predawn hours that January morning. I was comfortable in just a sweatshirt and jeans and Lori was in crisp, light blue pajamas. We settled her into a wooden swing and then I sat next to her. Lana placed a little plastic bowl holding a few saltines in her sister's lap and left us alone as I turned on my laptop.

And then Lori calmly and slowly did the hardest thing a mother can do: She said goodbye to her family. She dictated a different letter to each child, two sons and a daughter, her husband, and her sister. She told each one how certain attributes she loved in them would help them in life. She offered advice. She thanked them for what they had given her. I lifted a cup of apple juice after every few sentences, and she sipped drops of the liquid from a straw.

She died not long after that night. Andrew Meacham, the *Tampa Bay Times* obituary writer at the time, received numerous calls suggesting he write about Lori. I asked if I could track down one fact for his story and called Penguin Random House, the publisher of *Wonder*. When I explained why I wanted to know how *Wonder* had sold in Tampa Bay, a compassionate media relations rep called back within an hour. More books had sold in Tampa Bay than anywhere else in Florida, even though Miami was a much bigger market. In fact, more copies of *Wonder* had sold in Tampa Bay than in all of Florida combined. The sales could only be the result of my story about Lori.

Lori left many things to the many people who knew her, as well as to the thousands of kids who have no idea that Lori Crotts ever lived. If they read *Wonder* because of her, maybe they are a little nicer to someone who doesn't fit in or even an actual friend to someone who's different. Then there are the kids who are different; I hope they find some strength through August, the protagonist in *Wonder*. I know every time I pass Lori's former house and see where we sat that night on the wooden swing hanging from the live oak, I'm reminded to strive for her level of strength and compassion.

—◊◊◊—

17. Sending Fan Mail is Tacky

*M*y former pen pal, Oscar-winner Olivia de Havilland sued Hollywood hitmaker Ryan Murphy and the FX network, charging Murphy with false representation of her in his FX series *Feud: Bette and Joan*. She filed the suit at age 100.

The show depicted Old Hollywood and the clashing lives and careers of Bette Davis and Joan Crawford. Catherine Zeta-Jones portrayed Ms. de Havilland, who came off as a bit catty and gossipy. In her complaint, the elder actress stated neither Ms. Zeta-Jones or Mr. Murphy made any attempt to contact her to learn more about her friendship with Ms. Davis or Ms. Crawford or confirm any of the stories from the series. In the lawsuit, the two-time Academy Award winner best known for playing Melanie Wilkes in *Gone with the Wind* described herself as a "unique role model for multiple generations of actors and fans."

I am one of those fans.

"A woman who can merge the best qualities of Scarlett and Melanie within herself will be perfectly adapted for modern life," Ms. de Havilland told me in 1980.

She wasn't my first choice for a sixth-grade project on a living person I admired, and based on how smart she is, I now guess she realized this. She probably discerned by reading between the lines of the letter I scrawled on college-ruled paper that I would have rather written Vivien Leigh, who played Scarlett, if she was still alive.

But Ms. de Havilland was as gracious as Melanie Wilkes herself to my pushy requests for autographed pictures of Ms. Leigh or Clark Gable. I used the lame excuse that I wanted a tangible piece of the movie, which was the epicenter of my life at age twelve.

"I hope these few words will serve as a palpable souvenir of something you love so greatly," she wrote to me on thick, cream-colored stationery with a watercolor print of a volcano on the front.

I was truthful, at least, about being obsessed with *Gone with the Wind*, having read the 1,037-page book twice that year after seeing the movie on the Turner Broadcasting System channel. When my teacher, Ms. Corey, told the class we were writing a letter to someone we greatly admired, I knew my choices were within the pages of the 1936 book or the reels of the 1939 movie.

I wasn't going to write to a relative, because that was just a normal person, and I didn't care a single bit about local, state, or national politicians. Classmates who felt the same opted for former first ladies, astronauts, or Olympians. Not me. I wanted to write to someone who had a connection to *Gone with The Wind*.

My parents were pleased I was reading so much, but also concerned I was idealizing the pre–Civil War South. They reminded me of the heartbreak and abuse we watched in *Roots*, two years before I saw *Gone with The Wind*. The familial relationship between slaves and their owners that was depicted by Margaret Mitchell and movie producer David O. Selznick, was the exception to the rule, if it was even somewhat factual at all, they said.

As a pre-teen I grasped this serious misrepresentation somewhat, but what stood out to me the most at that naïve age was the romance, the passion, Scarlett's grit, and, of course, her clothes.

I couldn't do my project on author Margaret Mitchell, who won a Pulitzer Prize for her one-hit wonder, because she was killed at age forty-eight by a drunk driver in 1949. Ms. Leigh, who won an Oscar for playing the beautifully flawed Scarlett, died in 1967 at age fifty-three of tuberculosis. And Gable, who was the dashing Rhett Butler, whom I would judge all boys and men against for years to come, died at age fifty-nine of a heart attack in 1960.

So that left Olivia de Havilland. It was probably a note that my father included along with my letter to the actress that prompted her to respond to me at all. I don't know exactly what he wrote, but I can tell from her response to him that he acknowledged my preference for Scarlett, but said he was buoyed by the fact that I also loved Melanie.

"That Katherine Victoria, a Scarlett by nature, should regard so highly Melanie is a grand sign. . . . Scarlett's vigor, resourcefulness, and perseverance are such splendid qualities in their positive expression. And Melanie's compassion, generosity, and lovingness are gifts very precious indeed," she wrote to him in a letter separate from mine.

(While the letter I received from her home in Paris was on heavy stationery in a thick envelope lined with French stamps, the one to my dad was scripted on much lighter airmail paper. Ms. de Havilland wasn't about to waste too much money on postage for total strangers.)

My father asked her if it was difficult to play such a patient, forgiving character day after day. "I identified with Melanie out of an appreciation for the values she represented that seemed so threatened when I was growing up and so worth preserving," she wrote. "One way to keep them alive was to play the role. A real-life

Melanie I have once or twice encountered. My own daughter to my joy is not unlike her."

Along with stupidly requesting movie souvenirs in my letter, I did manage to also ask the actress what it was like to be in what many consider the greatest movie of all time.

"As to the experience of working in *Gone with the Wind*, it was a wonderfully happy one for me. I was deeply attached to the character of Melanie, who had a rare wisdom of the heart, and I looked forward each day to living her life during the hours of filming," she recounted.

"Furthermore, I surmised that *Gone with the Wind* might have an unusual destiny — that it might live longer than the year or two which was the fate of most movies of that day. The thought of being part of something which would endure was very fulfilling, even exhilarating."

Ms. de Havilland knows something about enduring. Though she didn't win the lawsuit against Murphy and the FX, she lived on her own in an apartment in Paris well after age 100.

The lawsuit against Murphy, who produced *Glee*, *American Horror Story*, and *Scream Queens*, wasn't her first strike against the mighty entertainment industry. In 1943, at age twenty-seven, she sued Warner Bros. Studios to get out of extra time tacked on to her seven-year contract because she took unpaid leave when presented with mundane movie rolls. After she sued, the court came out against the longstanding practice of holding actors hostage to long-term contracts.

The ruling, which became known as the "de Havilland Law," is still cited today in entertainment contract disputes.

It's clear Olivia de Havilland herself has a strong dose of Scarlett's "vigor" as she called it in the letter to my father. She also has humor and was known as a prankster in her Hollywood days. Remember when Rhett helped Scarlett escape Atlanta after she delivered Melanie's baby? He lifted Melanie from the bed and rushed her down the stairs to an awaiting carriage as cannonballs dropped all around them.

Well, behind-the-scene stories reveal that on the first take of that scene, Ms. de Havilland secretly tied a heavy piece of lighting equipment to her waist. When Gable, who was known for his ruggedness, tried to pick up the slight actress, he couldn't even budge her tiny frame.

If I'd known at age twelve all I know now about Ms. de Havilland, she would have definitely been my first pick above all the others.

—§§§—

18. Never Get A Tattoo

The issues with my heart started at age seventeen and ended when I was forty-six. I'm talking about medical issues, not all those other issues throughout life that weigh heavy on the heart or even break it. I don't think they ever end.

Living with erratic heart trouble and having a daughter born with heart defects taught me that a lot of medical problems also don't have exact answers and solutions. Still, our lives were saved several times by amazing doctors and the progress of medical research.

When a doctor told me the pulmonary valve leading to the lungs of my one-day-old daughter's heart was closed, but it could be opened with a balloon at the end of catheter threaded up through my baby's leg, I felt like I was watching some science fiction movie. I hate science fiction because it's not proven. This plan also sounded completely unbelievable. I asked the surgeon how in the world she would accomplish such a feat. She answered very matter-of-factly: "It's what I do."

The morning I learned Charlotte needed cardiac intervention I immediately felt guilty for two reasons.

First of all, the night before, I insisted my precious baby sleep in the hospital nursery so I could get as much rest as possible before going home with a newborn to a two-year-old daughter in fewer than forty-eight hours. I saw two nurses raise their eyebrows at each other upon hearing my declaration, because I was the only woman in the maternity ward since Lucy Ricardo who didn't insist her newborn miracle sleep at her bedside.

Twelve hours later when Charlotte was whisked away to intensive care after our pediatrician found an irregular heartbeat during a routine visit, I saw them exchange judging looks again as I started crying. My newborn daughter had a life-threatening birth defect, and I may have missed my only night with her.

The other reason for my guilt was because I was sure I had passed on a bum heart to this little baby since I had one of my own. My problems started at age seventeen when I was a counselor at Camp Seafarer on the North Carolina coast.

"I just threw up in the bathroom," I told a friend from the boys' camp down the river when I saw him at the Sanitary Fish Market in Morehead City, where the women's restroom no longer lived up to the restaurant's name.

"Are you hungover or did you eat more than your daily quota of twenty hush puppies?" he teased. Neither accusation was the case. I boarded the *Joy Boy*, which would take seventy campers and ten counselors back to camp a few miles up the Neuse River. We were returning from Long Cruise, the campers' one night away from the camp about fifty miles away.

Somewhere in the middle of the two-hour trip, my heart went berserk. I was sweating profusely and couldn't catch my breath. My co-counselors wrapped ice in towels and packed them around me as I was lying in a patch of shade on the deck of the *Joy Boy*. My chest grew tighter and tighter as my heart beat faster and faster. The Seafarer nurse was waiting for me at the dock when we reached camp and loaded me into her station wagon. We raced forty miles to the hospital in New Bern.

Within a few minutes of arriving with a heart rate of 220 beats per minute, two doctors shot a drug into my body that reset the pace of my heart.

My parents, meanwhile, weren't answering their phone at home in Raleigh because they were at the Grove Park Inn in Asheville with no idea any of this was taking place. It was pretty much impossible to be a helicopter parent in the 1980s without cell phones or the Internet or any desire from parents to monitor their offspring on a daily basis.

So, I went through all of this without family at my bedside at the hospital in New Bern, though Seafarer staff visited regularly.

Three days later, I returned to camp with a heart monitor. Every evening when I showered, (I wore a swimsuit as all counselors did with little girls around) the ten-year-olds in cabin fourteen fought over who got to stand two feet beyond the stream of water and hold the recording component of the monitor that was tethered to my chest.

A week later, without any more problems, my co-counselors Ellen and Hilburn took turns carrying the monitor high above their heads on our day off as we waded out to the annual sandbar party at the beach. Yes siree, I had quite the conversation starter with wires attached to my well-tanned upper body and extending through the armholes of my American flag tank suit. Nothing says footloose and fancy free quite like a heart-monitoring device.

By summer's end the monitor found my heart was beating completely normally. With no other episodes, that tachycardia was blamed on exhaustion combined with mitral valve prolapse, which occurs in 6 percent of all women. I took a blood thinner for six months, checked in with a cardiologist every year for the next decade, avoided caffeine and cocaine, and had no further complications until I was forty-two.

That's when, on a sunny October Sunday, I joined about thirty of my dad's relatives at The Depot restaurant in Surry County, N.C. Before the biscuits even arrived, I started pouring sweat and my heart was racing. The hostess couldn't find a pulse because my heart was beating so fast. Within minutes, an ambulance arrived, and the paramedics decided they had to treat me right there in the parking lot because there wasn't enough time to make it to the hospital. My dad climbed in the front seat next to my cousin Lynn while every other Snow as well as fifty more diners from The Depot crowded around the ambulance.

The paramedics shot a wonder drug through an IV that made its way to my racing heart.

"This is like when your computer is messed up and you turn it off, then turn it back on, and it starts working fine. It's a reboot," one of the paramedics explained.

Lo and behold, my heart stopped for a fraction of a second and then started up on its own at a much slower rate. It was still higher than it should be, however, so I was raced fourteen miles along winding mountain roads to Hugh Chatham Memorial Hospital in Elkin. On the way, I looked through the back windows of the ambulance and saw a snake of Buicks and pickups following closely behind. Every one of the Snows from The Depot, plus more who were just getting out of church and had been alerted to the situation, were following the ambulance like a funeral procession. I called Adam, my husband at the time, who was in Florida, to fill him in.

He was worried, of course, but knew the true danger was over, so like any father taking care of three kids under ten on his own for the weekend, he leapt at the chance for a little help.

"I'm about to go to the grocery store," Adam said. "What should I get to go in their lunchboxes tomorrow?"

"Are you kidding me? I am in an ambulance on the way to the hospital. My heart was just stopped. And rebooted. I am in an ambulance. I am officially off Mom Duty," I said, but quickly added, "Actually, I think we do need peanut butter. Smooth, low sugar."

Five of my cousins talked their way into the emergency room to assemble around my dad and me. I was waiting to go through a battery of tests, but was out of danger at this point, so this time at Hugh Chatham Memorial Hospital is actually a very fond memory of family togetherness.

"I feel just terrible," my cousin Anne Marie said. "She spent last night with me and seemed fine. This morning all we did was go for a walk and then have some waffles."

"Waffles, Anne Marie? *Waffles?*" my cousin Mike said incredulously, tongue fully in cheek. "Is that what you people in Yadkin County call your uppers, or your downers, or whatever the drug *du jour* is these days? *Waffles?*"

Mike hailed from Surry County and like all Surry County residents who claim Andy Griffith and the Blue Ridge Mountains as part of their DNA, he made a point of looking down on neighboring Yadkin County as well as every other county in the state, nation, and world.

My sweet father, who was eighty-six at the time, was probably in more cardiac distress than I was by the time we all congregated in that emergency room. My health was his biggest concern, of course, but being a frugal Snow, he also worried what it was going to cost to change my flight back to Florida since my little stay in the hospital would prevent me from leaving later that night.

"Uncle A.C., I'm going to take care of it. If I have to, I'll put the doctor on the phone and send the airline Katherine's EKG. I'll make sure they don't charge a big change fee," my cousin Lynn said. "I know how to get things done. I keep saying I'm going to start a business called Rent a Bitch, so you are my first customer, and I'm going to charge you my friends and family rate."

A few minutes later she had cancelled my flight back to Florida and was booking a completely different one for $35 less than what I paid originally.

"Uncle A.C., I just need your credit card number so I can make the change," she called across the emergency room crowded with Snows and nurses but not yet a doctor. He announced the row of sixteen digits.

"Uncle A.C., I've been meaning to ask you something for a while," my cousin Tim chimed in. "What's your Social Security number? And what's your mother's maiden name?"

"You rascal," my dad said, smiling for the first time in hours.

When I did finally return to Florida, I wore a heart monitor for a few weeks, and it found no irregularities. Then I had another tachycardia two years later on a Friday morning while sitting at my desk at the *Tampa Bay Times*. Then it happened again at my parents' dining room table three weeks after that.

There was no heart monitor called for this time. My cardiologist said that based on the increasing frequency of the episodes, there was a rogue track in my heart's circulatory system causing unusual increases in my heartbeat. I needed a procedure to fix it as soon as possible.

A camera went up through an artery in my left leg while a catheter went up the right leg. The doctor watched an image of my beating heart on a TV screen and led the catheter to burn off the imposter pathway.

I really wasn't that nervous when it was my turn because I'd seen this crazy science fiction at work so many years earlier when Charlotte was a baby and Dr. It'sWhatIDo opened a valve in her heart, which was the size of a mini Reese's cup at the time. And again, when Charlotte was five, a different doctor would also thread a catheter and a camera into that same heart and place a Gore-Tex patch in the hole in her septum.

If the hole had been repaired at her birth, she would have needed open-heart surgery. But since it wasn't life-threatening, the doctor who fixed her valve watched it for a while in hopes the hole might grow together on its own. Five years later, however, the hole was expanding instead of closing, and it was time to fix the problem. The surgery was done at Duke University Medical Center by an acquaintance I knew in high school. The last time I'd seen him, he was buying beer with a fake ID. Twenty years later, he was guiding a camera and a catheter through my daughter's heart with amazing precision. The surgery was on Good Friday. By Easter, Charlotte was collecting eggs in my parents' backyard in Raleigh and the only traces of the ordeal were Band-Aids on each of her sturdy legs where the catheters entered her little body.

Shortly after becoming editor of *Bay* magazine, I met the local marketing director for the American Heart Association and told her why I was forever indebted to all the research and medical expertise in cardiology. Thus, it was hard to say no when she asked if Charlotte and I could be the subjects of a video telling the story of how we both survived multiple cardiac problems thanks to advances in medicine and research. We'd also be the guests of honor at the Go Red for Women luncheon with 500 people who would see the video that tugged at their heartstrings and wallets.

Nothing has ever stood between a microphone and me, but Charlotte took more persuading.

"Your second procedure when you were five left you with a completely fixed heart and just two Band-Aids," I told her. "If that had been done a couple years earlier you would have had to have open-heart surgery with a major scar and broken sternum. The research that the American Heart Association developed found a way to patch the hole without all that. If telling our stories can help raise money for more progress, we need to do it."

"You're making me feel so guilty," she said. "But I don't want to have so many people watching me talk about this. And I've got to finish all my college applications, and I don't want to be stressing out about being in a video."

"Okay, Charlotte. You do this video and say five sentences at the luncheon. You and a few friends do the next Heart Walk. You have a bake sale at church and raise $100. Guess what? You can add 'Student Ambassador for the American Heart Association' to your college resume."

"Okay. I'll do it. And not just because of my resume," she said.

We soon learned there would be eight to ten hours of filming to make a four-minute video. Even *I* wasn't ready for that much camera time.

The young video director asked me to look out our living room window with a pensive expression while caressing Charlotte's kindergarten journal where she'd drawn a picture of herself in a blue hospital gown with a bright red heart on the left side. It was twelve years past her procedure, and she was a healthy teenager, but I had to reenact the pain and fear I felt when she was born and again when she was five. I also had to sprinkle in the stories and fear of my own heart problems.

The melodramatic introductory scene was forced, but it was honest. Then Charlotte and I learned the definition of B-roll, the footage shown while we talked out of sight of the camera. She was filmed doing all of her hobbies—playing lacrosse, painting at an easel, making vegan chickpea burgers, and messing around with our mutt, Charlie.

"Uhh, I don't really have any hobbies," I tried to explain to the very talented twenty-six-year-old videographer named Vee who possessed a lot of camera equipment and no concept of life as a working mom of three. "I go for a two-mile walk with a friend or two a few times a week. Can you film that? It's really pretty with the sun coming up over Tampa Bay in the background."

"Well, we need something more visual. What do you do in your free time?"

"Sleep? Drink wine?" I offered.

"That's it?"

"Sometimes I read for a few minutes, before I sleep."

Vee looked at me kind of sadly. I knew what he was thinking.

"If your heart is so healthy and raring to go, why aren't you climbing rocks, running marathons, or at least refinishing shabby chic furniture? Why aren't you doing something more visual than sleeping, walking, and reading?"

After disappointing Vee, and myself, I was in a bad funk for a few days thinking I had to take up karate or start a nonprofit that would change the world. I told a good friend I'd come face to face with how I waste my limited hours of free time, and she offered another viewpoint.

"Katherine, you're always meeting someone for coffee, or a walk, or drinks on the Vinoy hotel porch. Who else schedules calls with high school friends or cousins when you have a free hour to go for a walk on a Sunday afternoon? Your hobby is people."

Okay. I'll take it. Having "people" as a hobby doesn't get my body in kick-ass shape, but it does enhance my life. Two of those people I make a special effort to stay close with came to the luncheon to see Charlotte and me on the big screen and teared up when Charlotte, the reluctant star, brought down the house.

"I'm glad that everything worked out because I couldn't imagine coming home from school and never seeing you or never hearing your voice again," Charlotte said in the video to me as we awkwardly leafed through her kindergarten journal. "Going through the same journey with heart disease has brought us closer. Knowing that makes our bond really strong because we have both been able to go through really tough times and make it through," she added.

I didn't know then that these sweet yet strong words would soften the blow two years later when she came home from her gap year of working abroad with a tattoo. It wasn't a butterfly on her lower back or a four-leaf clover on her left shoulder blade. She wasn't even sure she was getting one until she looked through the book and saw the little heart with a hole in the middle.

"That's how I always explain why I had to have heart surgery, because I was born with a hole in my heart," she told me after raising her shirt for a few seconds and flashing me the tatt. It's about the size of a Kennedy half dollar on the far-left side of her upper rib cage.

I was shocked. I was scared my parents would find out. And I completely and absolutely loved her.

"Well, Charlotte, at least it has real meaning. It's a sign of your resilience."

"I thought of that exact same thing as I was getting it."

If my older daughter gets a tattoo, and she probably will because she doesn't like her younger sister one-upping her, it will be at least twice as big. I hope it will symbolize her brilliant resilience as well.

I'll never get a tattoo. That's one rule I know I won't break. But I have one etched in my mind. It's Carolina blue, American Typewriter font, and simply reads: "Resilience."

19. Miranda Lambert is Not a Licensed Therapist

⟡⟡⟡

Miranda Lambert was far from the final nail in my marriage. Nobody, not even my closest confidants, went on record saying after twenty-four years of matrimony, it was over. The country singer, however, helped me understand why some relationships have reached their end.

In her song "Baggage Claim", she sings about suitcases that she's incredibly tired of carrying because she can't get a grip on them and they keep getting heavier.

In "Dead Flowers", she tells the story of a husband who doesn't notice the shriveled-up flowers in the vase of gray water. He tells her how beautiful they are but seems distracted. She sings of Christmas lights left on the house in January and a car that keeps rolling when the tires are threadbare.

In "Unhappily Married", Ms. Lambert sings from the perspective of a wife telling her husband all the things they both find wrong in their marriage, then asks why break up? They've made it this far, might as well keep going.

In "Tin Man", she offers advice to the *Wizard of Oz* protagonist. Having a heart really isn't that great. Love is hard. She'd happily take his armor if he wants her heart, scars and all.

I married the right person. I felt so lucky that a guy from New York City and a girl from Raleigh somehow crossed paths in Spartanburg, S.C. Even with our different backgrounds, we had so much in common. From our first date on, we never ran out of things to say.

That's how millions of relationships start. But we stayed immersed in each other long after courtship, marriage, and babies were born. When we drove eight hours between Tampa and Fripp Island, S.C., several times a year, we talked constantly, pausing only to change Disney videos for kids in the backseat or refill sippy cups. We never even turned on the radio.

We got married in Raleigh and moved to Tampa knowing nobody except two bachelor friends from my high school. Our first holiday season, I invited them for a formal dinner with the fine china and Waterford crystal we'd received as wedding gifts. Adam made a delicious and complicated Thai pasta from a *New York Times* recipe. Matt and Lee showed up more than an hour late. Drunk. But they said it was the best peanut butter spaghetti they'd ever tasted.

I slightly knew another woman from college and invited her and her husband over for dinner several times, but they weren't available. After my third invitation, she spelled it out.

"We have a lot of weekend friends. We are not going to be available on a Friday or Saturday for you. But maybe we could try something during the week," she suggested cheerfully.

I didn't call her again.

Because Adam and I were two people alone in Tampa, we grew even closer.

After six years of marriage, we moved to a great neighborhood in St. Petersburg with brick streets and big, shady trees.

Charlotte was a newborn and two-year-old Olivia was thrilled to have a towering live oak on which to hang a swing. There were none sturdy enough in the spanking new, antiseptic planned community we'd left behind in Tampa.

A college friend introduced us to lots of families with small children and the network I'd longed for took shape. We were on a busy circuit of toddler birthday parties and dinners with friends. I finally ran into people I knew at the grocery store and had plenty of "in case of emergency" contacts to list on those blue forms submitted at the beginning of every new school year.

Adam covered the city of St. Petersburg for the daily newspaper, then called *The St. Petersburg Times,* and I wrote the paper's weekly parenting column called *Rookie Mom.* My oldest daughter, Olivia got a little confused and told her friends I worked for Pokémon.

One hectic morning after Wade was just born when all three kids needed something at once and Adam was packing to go out of town, the *Today* show ran a segment on empty nesters. Marriage therapists offered tips for couples who find themselves lost after kids leave for college.

"We will have no problem as empty nesters," I remember saying.

"None at all," he said, as he kissed me goodbye.

If we had just a mediocre relationship from the start, maybe it could have survived evolving into worse than mediocre.

Life went on. Kids got older. Stuff happened. Baggage accumulated. We argued. We gave cold shoulders. We got lost in work. We got lost in kids. We disconnected. Something broke the ice. We laughed. We reconnected. Then stuff happened again. New baggage was packed on top of old baggage. And so on, and so on.

Whenever I felt we were in a really tough cycle, I'd suggest marriage counseling and Adam agreed every time. That's more than a lot of husbands do.

Most counselors, whether in their nondescript professional buildings or bungalows converted into offices they shared with acupuncturists, made the same suggestions.

Don't say "you always" or "you never."

Repeat your partner's statements to make sure you are interpreting him or her correctly.

Use "I statements." For example, "When I speak to you and you don't respond, I feel like you don't think what I say matters." Or "when you leave notes reminding me to take out the trash, I feel like you think I don't help enough around the house."

My cousin Lynn remembered the "I statements" from her rounds of marriage counseling before her divorce. She ended up saying, "When you act like you do, I feel like you are an asshole."

In and out of marriage counseling and life's stresses, Adam and I experienced good days and good weeks when we finished each other's sentences and made each other laugh. Then we'd have days and weeks when we couldn't walk the dog in the morning without an exchange that ended in silence or one racing ahead of the other to leave for work without saying goodbye.

We were both conscious of how we acted in front of our kids. When they worried about arguments or tension, we told them that it's a normal part of marriage, which is very true. But to my closest friends, I confided it wasn't normal for *our* marriage. We had been so happy and compatible and then we just weren't. One day I looked back at the past few years and saw we had become a roller coaster, Himalaya, or (insert your carnival ride metaphor here).

I went from missing Adam terribly when he traveled to being relieved when he told me he had to go out of town for work. When I got home from the office and saw his car already there, I rolled my eyes. I told him this and he admitted he often felt the same way. We started seeing our sixth marriage counselor in 2017 with the goal of putting our baggage on the table, sorting it all out, and getting back on solid ground.

We saw a man we both liked relatively well from January to June. Not much changed. We saw another counselor in the fall.

This seventh therapist told us that seeing six prior marriage counselors meant nothing if they weren't good. We liked him. He was direct with pointed questions. He tried to get to the roots.

Of all the therapists I'd written checks to in my lifetime, however, be they psychologists, psychiatrists, or licensed social workers, he was the only one who directed me to make it out to "Dr. So-And-So."

After an uncomfortable therapy session, I told a funny story to Adam to break the silence as we drove together back to work. I remembered another PhD who insisted on being called a doctor. He taught public speaking with my mother at North Carolina State University.

The speech department went to a convention at a Wrightsville Beach hotel, which was still old school enough that guests signed a register when checking in. My mother's PhD colleague, who was one of several with that distinction, signed in as Dr. James Bucknell while everyone else used only first and last names.

On the second day of their conference, a three-year-old girl staying at the hotel was stung multiple times by a jellyfish. Her parents dragged her little body out of the water and up on the shore as hotel employees ran up and down the beach bellowing for Dr. Bucknell. The good doctor rushed to the scene and rubbed a handful of sand on the welts rising on the girls' legs and suggested she take some aspirin. It was all in a day's work for a speech professor.

When I finished recounting the story to Adam, he laughed and told me I was a great storyteller and I kissed him. By the time we went to bed that night we were completely irritated with each other and I slept in our guest room, like I did on many nights.

A week later, we went back into marriage therapy. More unhappiness poured out on the doctor's cluttered desk. Nothing the PhD said or we said seemed to lessen the flow.

"We don't have a great marriage. A lot of the time it's pretty bad," Adam explained. "But sometimes it's okay. I feel like we could muddle through."

That's when I decided our marriage was over. I wasn't going to muddle through on a roller-coaster ride with valleys growing deeper if there was no hope of getting off.

Telling our children and seeing them struggle to adjust to divorce was harder than the worst scenarios I'd imagined. At the time of this writing, my parents have been married sixty-two years and still live in the house where I grew up. My children have to deal with things I never faced. Adam and I get along well, so that helps. Still, I keep mental lists of high-functioning, seemingly happy people who are children of divorce to remind myself that my kids will be okay.

I do know that I am okay. Wonderful friends and family have enveloped me when needed. I feel safe at home alone on the nights I don't have kids around. When Uber drivers deliver me from the airport to my dark house, I tell them I can't wait to get inside and see my two wild dogs, Scylla and Charybdis. (I really have a mutt named Charlie who adores anyone crossing the threshold or breaking through a window.)

I told a friend of mine who has had serious relationships, but never married, that I thought of her when I pictured a life with an uncertain future because she has lived one of the most full and happy lives I know.

"All I can say is that until I was about fifty-five or sixty, people sort of went 'awww' and felt sorry for me when I said I wasn't married. Since then I've experienced nothing but envy!" she replied in an email, adding: "I've always thought nothing would be greater than a great marriage though, and there are some out there."

This helped. So does my favorite song by Miranda Lambert.

It's called "All Kinds of Kinds". I don't have the rights to include any of her very beautifully astute lyrics. But I think the title speaks for itself.

—§§§—

20. Snoopers Never Prosper

After I got divorced, the thought of going on a date with some-one was intimidating. The last time I'd been on a date with someone new, Madonna was voguing, Macaulay Culkin was home alone, and Lori Loughlin was still just sweet Aunt Becky.

A few friends set me up on dates that went nowhere. I met one man after work for a drink, and he told me that he realized my children would always come first in our relationship before I'd even finished one glass of wine.

A date with another man was going well until he told me he had always been against gay marriage, but it was the law of the land now he had to respect what the Supreme Court decreed. Though I am a Democrat, I could date a Republican, but not someone who seemed to think tolerance meant accepting gay people have the same rights as everyone else only when the Supreme Court mandates it.

I actually did have dinner with a Republican who was even a generous GOP donor. I liked him enough that I Googled his name when I got home and found an article about his ex-wife's claims that he had an armory of guns, and she felt threatened when she agreed to their divorce settlement. It seemed like she was trying to get more money out of him, and the situation was ripe for exaggeration or total lies. Maybe there was no armory, but where there's smoke, there could be an AK-47.

After this string of non-starters, a friend's husband suggested he fix me up with his buddy who was an investment banker with a great sense of humor. Money and laughter sounded like a good combination, so I was all in. Turns out the funny banker was already dating a beautiful young ax thrower who performed at Ferg's sports bar in St. Petersburg.

I dated a college professor for a little while who was a smart conversationalist and liked gourmet restaurants, art shows, and intriguing plays. We had plenty in common even though he was twelve years my senior. I'd been warned that the second time around in the dating world, men prefer women ten or fifteen years younger so therefore, women tend to date men who are ten to fifteen years older.

After we'd been going out a few times a week for about a month, I met him after work one night for dinner. He was sitting at the bar, had already ordered a nice glass of chardonnay for me, and kissed me when I arrived.

He knew my favorite wine and was kissing me in public. "This man really likes me," I thought to myself.

After dinner, my date excused himself to go to the bathroom and left his phone sitting at the bar. I looked at it and started wondering what he was texting right before I walked in the door.

Maybe it was: "I'm about to meet the most amazing woman for dinner," or perhaps, "This chick knows how to chow down." I picked up the phone thinking it was probably locked, but when it wasn't, I decided to quickly see if I could find out what he really thought about me. As soon as I started scrolling, I realized I was about to cross a serious line, plus he could walk out and catch me at any second. I set the phone down and patted myself on the back for resisting the temptation. He reemerged, suggested we split one more glass of wine, then held my hand as we walked to my car.

When Friday arrived and I hadn't heard from him in three days, I texted to touch base. I read his reply silently while sitting in a meeting with a friend at the PR firm where I worked at the time.

"When I came out of the restroom the other night, I saw that my phone had been moved. I had taken the passcode off and could tell someone had looked at my texts. I have tried to think of any possible explanation for this but can only come to the conclusion that you were snooping through my life."

I wanted to throw up. My throat started swelling. My eyelids were sweating.

"What's wrong?" my co-worker, Leah, asked.

"I'm so embarrassed to even tell you. But I looked at the phone of the man I've been dating the other night but then put it down before I saw anything. I even went to sleep that night thinking how glad I was that I hadn't read anything. Now he's saying he knows I looked at it."

"Well," she said, with a long pause as her PR crisis management skills surveyed the situation. "Have you ever done this to anyone else?"

"No. I don't even read my kids' phones, even though that seems to be standard parenting procedure these days."

"Then tell him that. Tell him exactly what you just told me," she advised. "He'll believe you. He knows what kind of person you are."

I texted my explanation but still hadn't heard back several hours later when I Ubered to Ferg's sports bar where friends were gathering to watch UNC play Auburn in the 2019 NCAA Basketball Tournament. I called a friend in Raleigh on the way to the bar and tearfully told her what happened.

"He was testing you," the young Uber driver wearing a bikini said when I ended my call.

"What do you mean," I asked.

"Guys do that to see if we're crazy. It's a test. They think all women are crazy."

These were such wise words coming from a young girl wearing a bikini and driving strangers around in her car.

"You know, you might be right. Because I've seen him type in his passcode to open his phone plenty times. Why would he suddenly take it off and leave it at the bar?"

"Exactly, honey."

"And how did he know his phone had been moved?" I continued. "It may have been one inch further from his wine glass, but it's not like I put it in his seat, on the other side of his plate or stuck it in the shrimp tacos."

"He set you up, girl. Women may be crazy, but men are just cruel."

When I met my friend Whitney at Ferg's, I shared the Uber driver's theory. She thought it seemed far-fetched and assured me he was just disappointed but would get past this. At the end of the third quarter, when the Heels were starting to falter, I received a reply to the text I'd sent five hours earlier.

"This isn't working for me. We had some fun. We should go our separate ways."

I showed it to Whitney while the crowd around us erupted in cheers and moans as Auburn pulled ahead of UNC. Her big blue eyes got even bigger.

"I think the Uber driver is right," she yelled into my ear so I could hear her over the crowd as she squeezed my hand. "It's a good thing you looked at his phone because it brought this to a close sooner than later."

One of the perks of being divorced with mostly married friends is I can get their husbands' male perspectives. By 11:00 a.m. the next morning, my friends were offering up wise words from their menfolk.

Julian said he'd be more flattered than annoyed if a younger, good-looking woman liked him enough to look on his phone to find out what he was thinking.

Jimmy thought the professor was overacting, and I shouldn't

try to explain myself anymore. This guy needed to think about how he treated me.

Emery's reaction: "Are you kidding me? Moveon.org."

Another friend compared the man to Kathy Bates in *Misery*. "Remember when James Caan is trying to escape and he knocks over this little china figurine on the table, then he puts it back as he hears her coming in the door," she recounted. "Kathy Bates notices it's moved like half a millimeter and freaks out."

I shared the Phonegate fiasco with a friend in North Carolina who is a few years ahead of me in the world of divorce.

"The phone is an excuse," Sam said. "He'd already decided what he was doing. He wanted to end things."

"Well, what if I hadn't looked at it?"

"He'd have found some other reason, but I'm guessing it still would have been your fault," he said. "Good riddance."

A few days later, I ran into a friend who had a hand in getting the professor and me together and told her how things had played out.

"What night was it that you looked at his phone," she asked.

"Tuesday."

"Katherine, we saw him at a Rays game with a date the next night. They seemed pretty cozy. She was a lot younger."

"Younger than *me*?" asked the 51-year-old who saw herself as arm candy to a 63-year-old.

"Uh, yeah. Like late-twenties or early-thirties."

I updated Sam on the latest development.

"Damn. That's not even close to the rule of half," he replied, then explained the litmus test he and his single male friends follow as a guideline for dating younger women.

"Say you are twenty-six years older than your oldest child, divide that in half and you get thirteen. That means you don't date anyone more than thirteen years younger," he explained. "The rule makes sure anyone you date is closer to your age than your children's age."

I went from remorseful to riled. Damn riled.

Yeah, I was hurt that he chose some young thing over me, but more than that I was mad that he acted as though I was such a menace to society while he set me up and didn't have the nerve to just end things honestly.

I emailed the good professor and suggested we have a quick call or meet for coffee to clear the air. He agreed he didn't feel good about how things played out and opted for coffee the next day.

I decided not to mention the other woman because I didn't want him to think that was my problem. It was more about how he reacted after I had a momentary lapse of judgment.

"I hate that all of this happened," I said, after a bit of small talk.

"It's okay. I think it's best we're just friends," he said from his high horse.

"Well, I made a mistake, I explained what happened and apologized for it. What's your explanation for casting me off in a text like I was some one-night stand?"

"I probably had that coming," he said with a nervous smile. "I guess I was just trying to save both of us from an awkward conversation. You definitely deserved more than that. I'm sorry."

"I think things were running their course anyway, but I'm glad we don't have this thing hanging out there and it won't be awkward when we run into each other again," I said.

"Me too," he said, motioning for the check.

"So, you don't think I'm some crazy, stalker, right," I said.

"No, I don't think you are a crazy stalker. Don't worry," he said with a laugh, followed by no attempt to acknowledge he made any mistakes.

"Okay, and I guess I don't think you're an asshole," I added.

I decided to take a break from dating for the next seventeen years or so, until Harry Connick Jr. crossed my path one night.

I was walking to the Vinoy hotel on St. Petersburg's waterfront, with my laptop in hand to work on this very book, when our eyes met.

"Sorry about all this," the Cajun crooner said, as he stepped out of an RV and motioned to about 100 people under spotlights shining on a little Florida bungalow. I suddenly remembered reading that he was filming a Hallmark movie with Katherine Heigl in the fair city of St. Petersburg.

"Oh, it's fine, as long as I get a cameo," I managed to say. He laughed as he walked up to the front porch for his next scene. I joined the crowd of gawkers gathered on the sidewalk.

"I heard Harry is staying at the Vinoy, but I think Katherine is staying out at the beach," one bystander informed the rest of us.

Exit Katherine Heigl, enter Katherine Snow Smith.

I pictured the scene playing out like a Nora Ephron romantic comedy. Harry stops at the bar on the Vinoy porch for one nightcap after a long day of filming and notices me a few seats away with my computer.

"Is this why you missed your cameo? Because you had to *work*?," he says to me with a half-smile as he takes a sip of his Brandy Milk Punch. (You can take the man out of NOLA, but you can't take the NOLA out of the man.)

"I'm not working, I'm writing a book. You're not the only creative genius at the bar," I reply dryly.

I put my extremely realistic vision on hold just long enough to Google: How old is Harry Connick Jr.?

Bingo! We were the exact same age. It had to be me!

I rushed to the Vinoy to set the scene. Then I had a terrible thought and stopped in my tracks to Google another question.

"Is Harry Connick Jr. married? Please God, no."

Google didn't hold anything back to let me down easy.

"Jill Goodacre Connick is an American actress and former model. She was one of Victoria's Secret's main models in the 1980s and early 1990s. She is married to Harry Connick, Jr. The couple has three children."

If it's not an ax thrower, it's a super model.

21. Always Know Your Date's Pedigree

~~~

*A*fter numerous nudges from friends, I finally tried online dating. I posted and messaged, swiped left and swiped right, and kept reminding myself of people who met their life partners on these sites, but it wasn't as easy as it looks in the commercials.

It did start out fun, at least, when I was creating my profile with three friends on my fifty-first birthday. We scrolled through my phone to find flattering photos for my profile. The one of me wearing jeans and a Brooklyn T-shirt said I was low key. The one of me in an embroidered tunic, laughing with my head back holding a glass of wine showed I was fun. The photo of me in my long, black, suede boots and an off-the-shoulder short dress was declared the sexy shot. We added my column photo from when I was editor of a magazine in which I'm wearing a dress with a Piet Mondrionish print to show I was artsy and smart. (Little did I know, I might as well have posted four photos sporting a nun's habit.)

As we began crafting the profile, I reminded my friends I had no hobbies, played no sports, and had traveled nowhere exotic in the past decade besides Columbia. (Columbia, S.C.)

"Come on, haven't you been hiking?" one asked me.

"Maybe I've been four times if you count walking down a dirt road to that keg party on somebody's ranch."

"Well, then, you are a hiker."

"And didn't you volunteer at that urban farm that grows vegetables for the food bank," somebody else reminded me.

"I did that twice."

"That's more than I've ever done. Put that down."

Finally, we crafted a few lines that we thought came off as smart, humorous, and interesting.

> *I'm a newspaper reporter turned public relations account executive. (Doesn't that sound corporate and impressive?) I'm a North Carolina native (Go Heels) but have been in Tampa Bay more than twenty years. (Yet, I still call the gulf the ocean.) I love hiking and volunteering at an urban farm that grows vegetables for food banks. I like old movies at Tampa Theatre, and new ones, too. I'm always up for a glass of wine on the Vinoy porch with friends, a music festival, estate sale or strolling Central Avenue's eclectic shops.*

I started with Bumble, which supposedly puts women in control because we choose who we want to be in our queue, then those lucky men are notified they can contact us. I set my parameters for an age range that included men ten years older or five years younger and started scrolling to add prospects to my queue.

It was a far cry from *People*'s Sexiest Men of the Year or even the *Tampa Bay Business Journal*'s weekly roundup of promotions and new hires. Actually, a number of men were attractive, it was what they said or the pictures they posted that were the red flags.

I scrolled past hundreds of photos of guys at the gym pumping iron or reclining on their bed holding a glass of bourbon with a come-hither smile. Bumble offers probing questions to answer when creating your profile such as: "Do you like the color red or orange more?", "Do you prefer salt or pepper?", and "If you bought a book, what would you do with it?"

Some men couldn't be bothered to answer the questions or write a two-sentence profile. They just post three pictures at the gym in a muscle-T that reads "Property of Daytona Beach Correctional Facility," and think that's all they need to do to get in a woman's queue, as well as other places I'm sure.

I wasn't looking for my soulmate, but I was interested in someone for more than their looks. Though I'm not going to pretend I'm so righteous, looks did matter, and I felt guilty every time I swiped left because of a beer gut, prematurely white hair or a balding head. In real life, many of my male friends have one or all of the above, yet are great husbands, great fathers, and loads of fun. Because I know them, I think of them as perfectly handsome. But when you know nothing about a person except that he prefers the beach to the mountains and would choose steak as his last meal, looks are a more discriminating factor.

I set the criteria men had to meet to land a coveted spot in my Bumble queue.

No photos at the gym.

No photos in bed.

No shirtless photos.

No visible tattoos.

No millennial-wanna-be beards.

A college degree.

And they had to have more than just photos in their profile.

After realizing every man between the ages of twelve and ninety is dabbling in some kind of facial hair these days, I took that one off the list. Finally, I had assembled ten men in my queue. Of those, only two "buzzed" me back to show their interest. That hurt. But I thought of more than fifty men I had discarded, so why shouldn't I be discarded, too.

After bolstering my confidence, I started a conversation with one of my potential dates. I learned where he worked and where his kids went to school and with a few clicks on Facebook saw that we had several mutual friends. I texted one of them to ask her what he was like and she quickly replied. "NO. NO. NO. He cheated on his first and second wife. DO NOT GO OUT WITH HIM."

Are you kidding me? The first guy I'm matched with is a repeat cheater.

I messaged the other guy in my queue who lived across the bay.

"So, are you from Tampa or did you move here like most people?"

"I moved here five years ago for work."

"Where do you work?"

"In Tampa."

Duh.

"I meant what is the job that brought you here?"

"Sounds like you are only into how much money I make. Sorry, this conversation is over."

Whaaattt? I started to defend myself then decided I didn't want to converse with somebody so ready to hate on me.

A few days later, I put another five men in my queue and only one "buzzed" me back, saying: "A journalist. Your smart and pretty. I can't wait to find out if we can go bumbling together." Even if I wasn't cringing at his misuse of "your," I couldn't overcome the "bumbling" comment. What did that even mean?

A few days later, I shared my depressing online debut with Sam, my friend from college who is a few years ahead of me in the world of divorce. He asked me to send him my profile.

"Wow. You like old movies? And new ones, too? That's shocking," he said sarcastically when he called with his critique. "And you like wine with friends? That's unlike any other woman

I've ever met. Let me guess, you are just as comfortable in heels at a cocktail party as you are in boots at a bar?"

"Shut up. What am I supposed to say?"

"And your photos. You look pretty, but they are all from the waist up. Guy are scrolling right past those. Even where I live, which has no beach, women post bikini shots. In Florida, I'm sure that's all they post."

"Women my age are posting bikini shots?"

"Women your grandmother's age."

"Well I'm not doing that."

"Okay. Then you have to make your profile really stand out. Let me take a shot at it."

Later that night he texted this:

> *I want to go to dinner with someone who appreciates wits over fake tits. I still drink Chardonnay, even though it's out and Rose is in. I work out but am not posting a photo to prove it. Don't need to see your gym pics either. I've been known to go on a hike but won't be climbing Everest anytime soon. I like indie movies at Tampa Theatre, but can also quote* **The Hangover**.

I posted my jazzed-up profile on another site called Hinge, because I didn't like making the first move on Bumble. I got quite a few reactions within an hour, and several men wanted to meet me that night, but they weren't my type.

One potential date started out sounding great. "I live in Florida but was raised in Louisiana, so I hope you don't mind if I open doors for you and insist on paying the bill. I'm a Cajun gentleman, but I still appreciate a strong, independent woman who speaks her mind. Full confession: I have Herpes." His admission was punctuated with a frownie-face emoji.

I read it aloud to a friend and her husband later that night, and they were smiling encouragingly until I got to the disclaimer.

"Well, Katherine, you told us your list of criteria," my friend's husband said. "And I don't remember hearing anything about you having a problem with venereal diseases." I genuinely respected the gentleman from Louisiana for being honest but ruled him out as my first match.

My profile continued to generate interest, but most of it seemed to be coming from men with tattoos of purple parrots on their shoulders or guys posing on all fours on cheetah-print sheets. "I haven't met anyone I'd leave my couch for yet, but at least my new profile is getting a lot of response," I told my friend Kate one night.

"Well, yeah, you're getting responses from these guys who want to meet you in an hour because you use the word 'tits.'"

"But I use it as in 'I don't have fake ones.' I have wits not fake tits."

"Katherine. They aren't that impressed with your clever rhyme. They see the word 'tits' on a dating website and think you can't wait to hand yours over. You've got to take that line out."

I did and the responses dropped dramatically. Finally, one nice looking man from Tampa messaged me, and we struck up a good conversation that lasted several days until he asked me to see *Phantom of The Opera*. I was going out of town that weekend but asked for a rain check. We texted more the next week, and he asked me to meet him for dinner Thursday night. By late afternoon that day I hadn't heard a word from him so I texted and suggested a couple places we could meet.

He never replied and I learned a new word: ghosted.

"He met somebody else he likes more," a friend in L.A. and veteran online dater informed me. "He ghosted you. It happens all the time."

She went on to tell me she pays to get a background check on every online date she makes. More than half the time, she learns the man is using a fake name and about one in three times she finds out they're married.

Cheaters. Facial hair. Ghosted. Fake names. Married men. Herpes. My confidence-shredding 20 percent "buzz" rate. I deleted Hinge and signed up for Hulu.

—⚬⚬⚬—

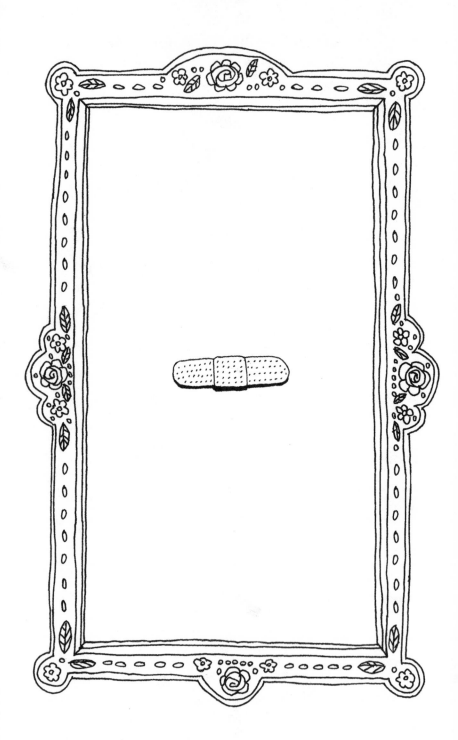

22. Never Let Them See Your Scars

❧

When things aren't going well, friends can say something that somehow breaks the tension to bring laughter and momentary relief. Other than dropping off a casserole, making someone laugh is sometimes the only thing they can do to help.

My former father-in-law, a wonderful man from Mobile, Alabama, choked to death during dinner at home with his wife and two friends. It was a terrible, desperate moment when the elderly male dinner guest tried to perform the Heimlich maneuver to no avail. Two days later the gentleman confided to my former mother-in-law that after her husband died that night, he asked his wife: "Do you think we'll be invited back?"

The exchange brought the first bit of laughter the newly dubbed widow had experienced in days.

Three years before I got divorced, there was a time when my husband and I were briefly separated, all three of my kids were dealing with stuff, and both my parents were in the same hospital in Raleigh. After I tucked my mom and dad into their respective beds two floors apart, I went to spend the night with my friend Beth. Her husband greeted me with a hug.

"What can I get you? Wine? Diet Coke? Maybe a gun?" he said flatly. I burst out laughing and the stress fell away for at least an hour.

I remembered his line when I was diagnosed with colon cancer last year. Over the past eighteen months, I'd gotten divorced, sold the house where my children grew up, left the newspaper where I'd worked for more than twenty years, started a new career and faced an uncertain financial future. My parents were aging. I was their only child living 700 miles away. My three kids were navigating divorce, high school, and college. All this and cancer were a lot to get through.

Fortunately, though, the cancer was caught early thanks to a colleague at my new job who was about thirty years old. As we walked to the parking lot one day after work, she asked me my age.

"You should never ask a woman a question that's answered in numbers," I replied with a laugh. "That goes for weight, bank balance, number of times down the aisle, and age."

She then explained her dad died of colon cancer, so she makes a point of reminding people to get a colonoscopy if they are fifty or older.

I was fifty-one at the time, so I scheduled my screening and found out I had cancer. My friend from work may well have saved my life, so I've taken up her same cause and now ask everyone in my age group if they are due for a colonoscopy. It's turned out to be quite the cocktail party fodder.

"Yes, I've had mine. And when I woke up afterwards the doctor told me I was quite combative during the procedure," my friend Louis shared. "I said, 'Damn right I was combative. You were putting a camera up my butt.'"

Another friend got a much better review from his gastroenterologist. "My doctor told me he could tell I took the cleansing of my colon very seriously and really appreciated that," Joe bragged. "I may not have many talents, but I can really cleanse my colon."

When my friends learned I would be in the hospital for five days after the tumor was removed and my intestines were restructured, they went into action, deciding who would take me to the hospital, who would be there when I came out of surgery, and who would stay with me at home while I was still recovering. Gift cards for Chick-fil-A and other restaurants for my kids piled up in our mailbox before I even went into the hospital. Care packages with soft blankets, magazines, and books arrived as well.

My friend Burchie told me she was on the hunt for a pretty nightgown and robe to give me until I reminded her I'd have to wear one of those lovely tie-in-the-back hospital gowns that could accommodate an IV.

"Well, then, I'm going to get you a bed jacket," she declared.

For any readers born after 1955, a bed jacket is a short jacket worn to cover the chest, shoulders and arms while sitting up in bed. Hollywood starlets in the 1930s popularized bed jackets by wearing elegant versions with feathers and lace when lounging in their boudoirs.

In a 1962 episode of *The Andy Griffith Show*, Aunt Bee wants nothing more for her birthday than a pretty bed jacket she spotted in a store window. Through a confusing turn of events, the mayor of Mayberry buys the bed jacket first as a gift for his wife, and Andy must trade his favorite and luckiest fishing pole to procure the jacket for Aunt Bee. He explains to Opie that Aunt Bee's happiness upon opening her gift means more to him than any fish he would ever catch.

"Burchie, you are so thoughtful," I told her, "but I think they quit making bed jackets about the time women were no longer required to carry a pot roast in order to be let out of the kitchen."

"Then I'll find St. Petersburg's Aunt Bee and borrow hers," she laughed.

So, all bases were covered down to the bed jacket, yet it was the first time since I got divorced that I felt utterly alone. Friends happily volunteered to be with me through every moment, but no one person had to be with me the whole time.

At my pre-op appointment, I filled out all the paperwork and listed a friend instead of a husband as the emergency contact. I checked "self" when asked repeatedly who was financially responsible. I checked the box labeled "divorced" instead of "married."

Why does that matter if I've already given my emergency contact? Do they offer speed dating in the recovery room?

And why was I slightly ashamed to check "divorced?" I guess I wanted to check the box that said, "Marriage ended after numerous marriage counselors, but we get along well for the sake of our children."

I left the appointment with a goodie bag containing this super-sonic-triple-anti-bacterial soap that I had to wash with the next morning before my surgery. It reduced the chance of infection. I cried on the way home for the first time since my diagnosis.

"I don't know why I'm suddenly terrified," I told a friend. "They caught it early, and I'll be fine. But if I have to use this soap to ward off infection, then it's like anything can go wrong."

"The soap made it real," she said. "This is real, Katherine. You can't control it. You just have to get through it and face whatever happens."

Later that afternoon, Burchie came by with a beautifully wrapped present. I don't think Aunt Bee was even half as thrilled as I was to open the white satin bed jacket. "I know it's the last thing you need or want. Don't even take it to the hospital," she said laughing. "Just know we're here for you."

I showed the bed jacket to my kids and tried to explain that it was this antiquated, ridiculous, hilarious thing that just made me laugh and feel loved. Wade, my most cold-natured child who regularly ranks blankets on their level of coziness, said he wanted his own bed jacket. He tried mine on and declared he was never taking it off.

The bed jacket was the last thing I packed in my little travel bag the next morning, before I washed with the soap. Instead of thinking of the cleansing as a last-ditch effort to prevent infection, I told myself it was a strong shield. I prayed for the surgeon's incredible mind and deft hands.

My friend Hope arrived at 5:15 a.m. to pick me up.

"Let's go kick this cancer's ass," she said when I opened the door. She insisted on carrying my bag as if I was already on bedrest.

Two more friends were allowed to join us in my curtained off pre-op alcove, and we laughed and talked like it was a girls' happy hour. Well, except I was the only one catching a buzz and instead of $6 Chardonnay, it was $6,000 anesthesia.

Soon their voices drowned into a low hum and a few hours later I woke up with the next shift of friends watching over me. My children came to visit late that afternoon, including Wade who had just gotten his driver's license that day. Nothing says teenage independence quite like driving solo to St. Anthony's Hospital to see your mom practice getting in and out of bed with a catheter hanging out of her gown.

When my friends and family weren't around, the hospital staff provided compassionate care and slices of reality.

"Is that a *bed jacket*? I didn't know they made those anymore," said Susan, my first night nurse. She had worked at Thalhimers department store thirty years earlier and remembered selling them. By the end of her shift, I'd learned that Susan's husband was shot in the head at age twenty when he was delivering a pizza, then a bullet fragment in his brain was shaken loose when he rode a roller coaster at Busch Gardens at age forty. Within hours, he was blind and by the end of the night he was dead.

Rose, the housekeeper, told me she arrived in St. Petersburg from Haiti a decade earlier as a seventeen-year-old in urgent need of open-heart surgery. When American doctors decided she needed continued medical care that wasn't available in Haiti, Rose moved in with a Haitian family in St. Petersburg that she'd never met and has only seen her parents once since then. They've been waiting ten years to emigrate.

Kevin, an ambulatory aid, came in twice a day to help me move around. He was from the Philippines and had immigrated to Florida a few years earlier with his wife. His excitement and praise in slightly broken English over every step I took as my abdomen healed, more than made up for coming in last in the duathlon at the beach. On my fourth day at the hospital, with no shower and tangled, matted hair, Kevin quietly whispered to me: "You want some comb Miss Katherine? I can get you some comb."

My roommate Lisa, who was dealing with an infected wound from a previous surgery, lived on the other side of the mauve curtain that divided our hospital room. It was not as romantic as the one that separated Clark Gable and Claudette Colbert in *It Happened One Night*.

She watched the ESPN Classic station while I binged on *Friends*. Occasionally Lisa flipped to cable news, which was obsessively reporting the curious jail cell suicide of accused pedophile Jeffrey Epstein.

"He didn't die. They killed his creepy little ass. Cause he was gonna' talk. He was naming names," she said with authority. I wasn't sure if she was speaking to me, to herself, or the newscaster, but I didn't want to appear rude.

"Yeah, but who did it? I bet a lot of people didn't want him to talk," I called out over the curtain.

Lisa went silent, and I sensed annoyance, as if I'd been listening in on a private phone call. She switched the channel back to the 2018 Peach Bowl between Florida and Michigan.

Before my operation, the surgeon said he couldn't predict how long I'd be in the hospital waiting for my intestines to start working again because my get-out-of-jail-free card would be a big, loud fart.

Yes, one of the most respected surgeons on Florida's west coast, freely used the word "fart."

My friends, the hospital staff, and I started Fart Watch within two days of my surgery. It was funny, small talk with Rose, Kevin, and Susan. But when the hospital doctors discussed my bowels like I had no idea what needed to happen, it was insulting.

"Have you passed gas yet, Mrs. Smith?" Dr. Alamante asked. (Clearly, he hadn't seen the check mark in the divorced box.) "Because you can't leave the hospital until we know your bowels are working."

"Now tell me Miss, Mrs., Msssss. Smith, have you passed gas yet?" Dr. Adler inquired. "Your wound is healing nicely, but you can't check out until we know your digestive system is back in action."

"Good morning, young lady," Dr. Dahari greeted me. "Now tell me, have you passed any gas? You need to pass gas before you can go home."

"No, I have not passed gas. But I fully understand the rules of the game. Y'all don't have to keep explaining it to me every time you stop by. I fully understand. I will tell you and everyone on this floor the second I feel one coming," I hissed, on day four of no food and no gas.

The next day, I passed gas. In fact, I passed gas three times and each time I called a nurse who excitedly informed all the higherups, including the charge nurse, the doctors, TMZ, and Pope Francis. Yet nobody with authority authorized me to start eating soft foods for almost twelve hours.

Finally, it was time to check out.

"You pray for me and I'll pray for you," Rose said, as we hugged goodbye.

My friend Page, from Charlotte, came to stay several days while I recovered. Along with regularly delivering meals and painkillers to my room, she cleaned out my refrigerator, picked out the dead flowers from the arrangements I'd received, washed and folded three loads of laundry, and made Jell-O. She also went on a Target run for basic provisions I needed to feel caught up on life including reading glasses, phone chargers, new underwear, and thank-you notes. I no longer felt lost without a husband.

A week later I learned the cancer had spread to only one of the fifteen lymph nodes sampled, and I didn't need chemo or radiation. I'll have screenings every year for quite a while.

When I visited Charlotte at college a couple months later, we shared a hotel room in Burlington, Vermont, and she caught sight of the scar running across the right side of my stomach as I changed clothes.

"Mom! That is so awesome," she said. "You should wear a midriff shirt so everyone can see it."

That would require a whole other procedure and I don't think my insurance covers liposuction. We all have wounds and scars we can expose or tend to alone. I choose to expose mine, because that's how you end up with bed jackets, one-liners, and support from friends through all the lows and the highs.

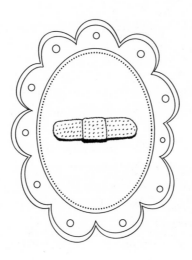

Afterword

$\mathcal{S}$everal months after my divorce, I approached an aisle seat on a flight to Raleigh and started to heave my heavy rolling suitcase into the overhead bin. The gentleman sitting next to the window jumped up and insisted on helping me.

I thanked him, then settled into my seat, put in my earphones, and hung out the do-not-disturb sign. I wasn't interested in a ninety-minute chat, though I did take note of his bare ring finger, having already mastered the skill of looking for the absence of that little gold band using only my peripheral vision.

After a while, I worried I was being rude and handed him a Southwest drink coupon when the flight attendant came through taking orders.

"Karma for helping me with my bag," I said, but kept my earphones in place and returned to my reading.

When the drinks arrived, he toasted me with his bourbon and ginger, and I decided I should at least make a little small talk. We had a good conversation about weather, kids, life, man's inhumanity to man. Normal stuff. When the topic of divorce came up, he was a veteran to my novice status and gave me perhaps one of the best pieces of advice I've received yet. I've shared his morsel of wisdom with friends in all stages of life many times since. One of those friends, a Pulitzer-Prize winning *Tampa Bay Times* reporter half my age, was leaving the paper to start a new job at the *Philadelphia Inquirer* recently. I hosted a going away party for her, and in an unexpected reversal of celebration protocol, she brought me a gift.

Inside the ornately wrapped box was a personalized wine glass with my flight companion's wise words etched onto the glass.

"There's a reason the windshield is bigger than the rearview mirror."

I make a point of choosing this glass whenever I finish an essay, land a new client, or simply book a flight to some exotic location like Charlotte, and toast the unknown that lies ahead.

Acknowledgments

Thank you to Stephanie D. who insisted I wear her shoes. Thank you to Margaret who told me several years ago to just start writing. Thank you to Stephanie Hayes, a great editor who found the string of broken rules running through these essays. Thank you to Sam, another great editor who was mildly helpful and humorous.

Thank you to SheWrites for believing in this book and all that they do for new writers. Thank you to Cathy for her great attention to copy editing. Thank you to amazing friends who were integral parts of these stories. Thank you to the staff at the Vinoy hotel who never laughed when I told them I was always on the front porch with my laptop because I was writing a book.

Thank you to Olivia for telling me ten years ago that a laptop was a better gift than jewelry because I would use it to write my book. Thank you to Charlotte for telling me her British friends cried when she read them the story about our hearts. Thank you to Wade for teaching me how to highlight a document and other complicated IT help all along the way. Thank you to my parents, the ultimate storytellers, for showing me how to observe and share life's moments, big and small.

About the Author

*K*atherine Snow Smith has lived throughout the South as a newspaper reporter, magazine editor, public relations executive, daughter, sister, mother, wife, divorcee, and friend. She graduated from the University of North Carolina at Chapel Hill and started her journalism career covering three miniscule towns in South Carolina. After a stint covering business in Charlotte, NC, she got married, moved to Florida and started a 20-year career at the *Tampa Bay Times*. She covered business, then, after having her first baby, started a parenting column called Rookie Mom. Now—three kids, two careers, and one divorce later—she's embracing the fact that life has many chapters.

Author photo © Patty Yablonski